GONDI GRAMMAR AND VOCABULARY

GONDI GRAMMAR AND VOCABULARY

HENRY DRUMMOND WILLIAMSON

Published by

FacsiMile Publisher
12 Pragati Market
Ashok Vihar, Ph-2
Delhi - 110052, India
Phone: 011-47034999
Email: www.facsimilepublishers.com
info@facsimilepublishers.com

Distribution Network
gyanbooks.com
India, USA, Canada, UK, Australia

ISBN: 978-93-3303-170-7 (PB)
First Published, 1889

2nd Impression 2025

Printed at: Gyan Press, Delhi.

GONDI GRAMMAR AND VOCABULARY
Author: HENRY DRUMMOND WILLIAMSON

GONDI GRAMMAR

AND

VOCABULARY.

BY

REV. H. D. WILLIAMSON, M.A.,

CHURCH MISSIONARY SOCIETY, MANDLA, C.P.

LONDON:

SOCIETY FOR PROMOTING CHRISTIAN KNOWLEDGE,

NORTHUMBERLAND AVENUE, CHARING CROSS, W.C.

GONDI GRAMMAR.

The Noun.

Gender.—The masculine gender in Gondi is used simply for the names of males: all other objects may be spoken of as neuter *or* feminine. It is difficult to decide under which name non-masculine nouns should be grouped; if the language be viewed from the stand-point of its neighbour, Hindi, they should be called feminine, but as one of the Dravidian languages it is more natural perhaps to view them as neuter.

Number.—There are two numbers, singular and plural: dual does not exist in Gondi.

Formation of the plural.

Rules.—(1) Add क *k* to the singular; ex., काल *kál*, a foot, plural काल्क *kálk*, feet.

(2) Add अंग *aṇg* to the singular, if the word ends with a long vowel, especially after double consonants; ex., पिट्टे *piṭṭe*, a bird, plural पिट्टेंग *piṭ-ṭeṇg*, birds; मट्टा *maṭṭá*, a mountain, plural मट्टांग *maṭṭáṇg*, mountains.

(3) If the word in the singular ends with the

consonant र *r* after a long vowel, the र *r* usually becomes ह्क *hk*; ex., मिआार *miár*, a daughter, plural मिआाह्क *miáhk*, daughters.

N.B.—A few which end with long vowels add ह्क *hk* in the plural, at the same time shortening the vowel; ex., मायजू *máyjú*, wife, plural मायजुह्क *máyjuhk*, wives.

Exceptions to the above rules:—

अल्ली *ullí*, a rat, plural अल्क *alk*, rats.
मर्री *marrí*, a son, plural मर्क *mark*, sons.
सर्री *sarrí*, a road, plural सर्क *sark*, roads.

The affix वाड़े *wáṛe*, people, plural वाड़ेर्क *wáṛerk*, people.

कल्ले *kalle*, a thief, plural कल्लेर्क *kallerk*, thieves.
दाऊ *dáú*, father, plural दाउल्क, *dáulk*, fathers.
पुड़ी *puṛí*, an insect, plural पुर्क *purk*, insects.
मामा *mámá*, father-in-law, plural मामाल *mámál*, fathers-in-law.
सिड़ी *siṛí*, a parrot, plural सिर्क *sirk*, parrots.

Declension.—Changes of the noun preparatory to forming the root for declension:—

(1) Some add the case-termination to the simple unaltered word; ex., पिंडी *pinḍí*, flour, पिंडी ता *pinḍí tá*, of flour.

(2) Some drop the final letter before the case-termination; ex., डोंगुर *ḍoṇgur*, jungle, डोंगुता *ḍoṇ-*

gutá, of the jungle; रोन *ron*, a house, रोते *rote*, in a house.

(3) Some drop the last two letters before the case-termination; ex., पाटांग *páṭáṇg*, songs, पाटाना *páṭáná*, of songs; मट्टांग *maṭṭáṇg*, mountains, मट्टाना *maṭṭáná*, of mountains.

Rules for Declension.

(1) Nouns which form their plural in क *k* or ह्क *hk* add to the root:—

	Singular.	Plural.
Genitive,	तोर *tor*, तोर्क *tork*, ता *tá*, तांग *táṇg*.	नोर *nor*, नोर्क *nork*, ना *ná*, नांग *náṇg*.
Dat. & Acc.,	तुन *tun*.	उन *un*.
Locative,	ते *te*.	ने *ne*.
Ablative,	ताल *tál*.	नाल *nál*.
Prep. root,	त *t*.	उन *un*.

The following, with many other words, follow this rule:—

मड़ा *maṛá*, a cow; लेंग *leng*, a voice; अल्ली *allí*, a rat; पुंगार *puṇgár*, a flower; नांगेल *náṇgel*, a plough; मेन्डुल *mendul*, a body; आर *ár*, a woman; रोन *ron*, a house; डोंगुर *ḍoṇgur*, jungle; मेस *mes*, an egg; नेल *nel*, a field; कुर्र *kurr*, a hen; तोल *tol*, skin; पीर *pír*, the stomach; सर्री *sarrí*, a road; नार *nár*, a field.

But notice (*a*) In नेल *nel*, कुर्र *kurr*, and तोल

tol, the त *t* of the inflection becomes द *d,* for the sake of euphony; as नेदे *nede,* कुर्दोर *kurrdor,* तोलदा *toldá.*

(*b*) In मर्री *sarri,* the same change is usually made; as सरदे *sarde,* सरदोर *sardor.*

(*c*) In पीर *pír* and नार *nár,* the त *t* of the inflection is hardened into ट *ṭ*; as पीटे *píṭe,* नाटे *náṭe.*

N.B.—नार *nár* also makes a genitive singular नाटेनोर *náṭenor.*

(2) A large class of nouns, chiefly ending in आल *ál,* change त *t,* the first letter of the usual case inflection, into न *n*: the case forms thus becoming:—

	Singular.	Plural.
Genitive,	नोर *nor,* नोर्क *nork,* ना *ná,* नांग *náṇg.*	The plural remaining as above, except that there is a vocative.
Dat. & Acc.,	न *n.*	
Locative,	ने *ne.*	
Ablative,	नाल *nál.*	
Prep. root,	न *n.*	
Vocative,	नी *ní.*	नीट *níṭ.*

So the following:—माड़साल *máṛsál,* a man; पेड़गाल *peṛgál,* a boy; मूंजाल *múṇjál,* a monkey; बीलाल *bilál,* a cat; अड़जाल *aṛjál,* a bear; गधाल *gadhál,* a donkey, &c.

Also:—पेड़गी *peṛgí,* a girl; मर्री *marrí,* a son;

मायजू *máyjú*, a wife; कल्ले *kalle*, a thief; मिआर *miár*, a daughter; सेलार *selár*, a sister; टाली *ṭálí*, a cow; तम्मुर *tammur*, a brother; फापे *pháре*, a butterfly.

(3) Nouns which form their plural by adding अंग *aṇg* to the singular, have नुंग *nuṇg* and न *n* for their case-inflections of the dat. and acc. plural, and plural prepositional root.

So the following:—आकी *ákí*, a leaf; पाटा *páṭá*, a song; पिट्टे *piṭṭe*, a bird; मट्टा *maṭṭá*, a mountain; छौवा *chhouwá*, a child; पन्ने *panne*, a frog; पद्दी *paddí*, a pig; नन्नी *nanní*, the loins; कची *kachí*, iron; दूदूं *dúdúṇ*, the breasts; कोड़ा *koṛá* a horse; साड़ी *sáṛí*, bread; अर्मी *armí*, a buffalo, &c.

Some examples of the declensions of nouns, to illustrate the above rules, are here given:—

	Singular.	Plural.
Nominative,	तम्मूर *tammúr*, a brother.	तम्मूर्क *tammúrk*.
Genitive,	तम्मूनोर *tammúnor*, नोर्क *-nork*, ना *-ná*, नांग *-náṇg*.	तम्मूर्कनोर *tammúrk-nor*, नोर्क *-nork*, ना *-ná*, नांग *-náṇg*.
Dat. & Acc.	तम्मून *tammún*.	तम्मूर्कुन *tammúrkun*.
Locative,	तम्मून्ते *tammúnte*.	तम्मूर्कने *tammúrkne*.
Ablative,	तम्मूनसे *tammúnse*, तम्मूनताल *tam-múntál*.	तम्मूर्कनाल *tammúrk-nál*, तम्मूर्कसे *tam-múrkse*.

	Singular.	Plural.
Prep. root,	तम्मून tammún.	तम्मूर्क tammúrk.
Vocative,	तम्मूनी tammúní.	तम्मूनीट tammúniṭ.

N.B.—The four forms of the genitive are used respectively when the governing word is in the masc. sing., fem. sing., masc. plural, and fem. plural.

	Singular.	Plural.
Nominative,	छौवा *chhouwá*, a child.	छौवांग *chhouwáṇg*
Genitive,	छौवातोर *chhouwátor*, तोर्क *-tork*, ता *tá*, तांग *-táṇg*.	छौवानोर *chhouwanor*, नोर्क *-nork*, ना-*ná*, नांग-*náṇg*.
Dat. & Acc.	छौवातुन *chhouwátun*.	छौवानुंग *chhouwánuṇg*.
Locative,	छौवाते *chhouwáte*.	छौवाने *chhouwáne*.
Ablative,	छौवाताल *chhouwátál*, छौवासे *chhouwáse*.	छौवानाल *chhouwánál*.
Prep. root,	छौवा *chhouwá*.	छौवान *chhouwán*.
Vocative,	छौवानी *chhouwání*.	छौवानीट *chhouwániṭ*.
Nominative,	मायजू *máyjú*, a wife.	मायजुःक *máyjuak*.
Genitive,	मायजूनोर *mayjunor*, नोर्क *-nork*, ना *-ná*, नांग *náṇg*.	मायजुःकनोर *máyjuaknor*, नोर्क-*nork*, ना-*ná*, नांग-*náṇg*.

	Singular	Plural.
Dat. & Acc.	मायजून *máyjún.*	मायजुःकुन *máyjuakun.*
Locative,	मायजूने *máyjúne.*	मायजुःकने *máyjuakne.*
Ablative,	मायजूनाल *máyjúnál,* मायजूनसे *máyjúnse.*	मायजुःकनाल *mayjuaknál,* मायजुःकसे *máyjuakse.*
Prep. root,	मायजून *máyjún.*	मायजुःक *máyjuak.*
Vocative,	मायजूनी *máyjúni.*	मायजुनीट *máyjúniṭ.*

Nominative,	दाउ *dáu,* brother (in a general sense).	दाउल्क *daulk.*
Genitive,	दाउनोर *dáunor,* नोर्क *-nork,* ना *ná,* नांग *náṇg.*	दाउल्कनोर *daulknor,* नोर्क *-nork,* ना *-ná,* नांग *náṇg.*
Dat. & Acc.	दाउन *dáun.*	दाउल्कुन *dáulkun.*
Locative,	दाउने *dáune.*	दाउल्कने *dáulkne.*
Ablative,	दाउनाल *dáunál,* दाउनसे *dáunse.*	दाउल्कनाल *dáulknál,* दाउल्कसे *dáulkse.*
Prep. root,	दाउन *dáun.*	दाउल्कुन *dáulkun.*
Vocative,	दाउनी *dáuní.*	दाउनीट *dáuníṭ.*

The Pronoun.

Personal Pronouns.

	Singular.	Plural.
Nominative,	नन्ना *nanná,* I.	मम्माट *mammáṭ.*

	Singular.	Plural.
Genitive,	नावोर *náwor*, नावोर्क *náwork*, नावा *náwá*, नावांग *nawáṇg*.	मावोर *máwor*, मावोर्क *máwork*, मावा *máwá*, मावांग *máwáṇg*.
Dat. & Acc.	नाकुन *nákun*, नाक *nák* (uncommon).	माकुन *mákun*, माक *mák* (uncommon).
Locative,	नाते *náte*.	माते *máte*.
Ablative,	नाताल *nátál*, नावाताल *náwátál*, नासे *náse*.	मावाताल *máwátál*, मासे *máse*.
Prep. root,	ना *ná*.	मा *má*.
Nominative,	इम्मा *imma*. Thou.	इम्माट *immáṭ*, इम्माड़ *immáṛ*.
Genitive,	नीवोर *níwor*, नीवोर्क *níwork*, नीवा *níwá*, नीवांग *níwáṇg*.	मीवोर *míwor*, मीवोर्क *míwork*, मीवा *míwá*, मीवांग *míwáṇg*.
Dat. & Acc.	नीकुन *níkun*, नीक *ník* (uncommon).	मीकुन *míkun*, मीक *mík* (uncommon).
Locative,	नीते *níte*.	मीते *míte*.
Ablative,	नीवाताल *níwátál*, नीसे *níse*	मीवाताल *míwátál*, मीसे *míse*.
Prep. root,	नी *ní*.	मी *mí*.

	Singular.	Plural.
Nominative,	ओर *or*, He.	ओर्क *ork*.
Genitive,	ओनोर *onor*, ओनोर्क *onork*, ओना *oná*, ओनांग *onáṇg*.	ओर्कनोर *orknor*, ओर्कनोर्क *orknork*, ओर्कना *orkná*, ओर्कनांग *orknáṇg*.
Dat. & Acc.	ओन *on*.	ओर्कुन *orkun*.
Locative,	ओने *one*.	ओर्कने *orkne*.
Ablative,	ओनसे *onse*.	ओर्कनाळ *orknál*.
Prep. root,	ओन *on*.	ओर्कुन *orkun*.

Nominative,	अद् *ad*, She, It.	औ *au*.
Genitive,	अद्देनोर *addenor*, अद्देनोर्क *addenork*, अद्देना *addená*, अद्देनांग *addenáṇg*, or तानोर *tanor*, तानोर्क *tanork*, &c., or अवेनार *awenár*, अवेनार्क *awenárk* &c.	अवेह्कनोर *awehknor*, अवेह्कनोर्क *awehknork*, अवेह्कना *awehkná*, अवेह्कनांग *awehknáṇg*.
Dat. & Acc.	तान *tán*, अद्देन *adden*, अवेन *awen*.	अवेह्कुन *awehkun*.
Locative,	अवेटे *awete*.	अवेह्कने *awehkne*.

	Singular.	Plural.
Ablative,	अद्देनसे *addense*, तानसे *tánse*, तानाल *tánál*.	अवेह्कनाल *awehknál*.
Prep. root,	तान *tán*, अद्देन *adden*, अवेन *awen*.	अवेह्क *awehk*.

Demonstrative Pronouns.

	Singular.	Plural.
Nominative,	एर *er*, This (masc.)	एर्क *erk*.
Genitive,	एनोर *enor*, एनोर्क *enork*, एना *ená*, एनांग *enáṇg*.	एर्कनोर *erknor*, एर्कनोर्क *erknork* एर्कना *erkná*, एर्कनांग *erknáṇg*.
Dat. & Acc.	एन *en*, एन्क *enk*.	एर्कुन *erkun*.
Locative,	एनते *ente*.	एर्कने *erkne*.
Ablative,	एनसे *ense*.	एर्कनाल *erknál*.
Prep. root,	एन *en*.	एर्क *erk*.
Nominative,	इद *id*, This (fem. or neuter).	इऊ *iú*.
Genitive,	इद्देनोर *iddenor*, इद्देनोर्क *iddenork*, इद्देना *iddená*, इद्देनांग *iddenáṇg*, तेनोर *tenor*, तेनोर्क *tenork*, &c.	इवेह्कनोर *iwehknor*, इवेह्कनोर्क *iwehknork*, इवेह्कना *iwehkná*, इवेह्कनांग *iwehknáṇg*.

Dat. & Acc.	तेन *ten*, इद्देन *idden*.	इवेह्कुन *iwehkun*.
Locative,	इवेटे *iweṭe*.	इवेह्कने *iwehkne*.
Ablative,	तेनसे *tense*, इद्देनसे *iddense*.	इवेह्कनाळ *iwehknál*.
Prep. root,	तेन *ten*, इद्देन *idden*.	इवेह्क *iwehk*.

The demonstrative pronouns ओर *or*, that (masculine); and अद *ad*, that (fem. and neuter); are declined as the personal pronouns ओर *or*, he, and अद *ad*, she, it. When used with nouns, however, theyare not declined; ex., एर मांड़साळोर *er mánṛsálor* "of this man"; इद नातेनोर *id nátenor* "of this village."

Indefinite Pronouns.

	Singular.	Plural.
Nominative,	बोरे *bore*, Anyone (masculine).	
Genitive,	बोनोरे *bonore*, बोनई *bonaí*.	
Dat. & Acc.	बोनई *bonaí*.	
Locative,	बोरेते *borete*.	Unused.
Ablative,	बोनइसे *bonaise*.	
Prep. root,	बोनई *bonaí*.	
Nominative,	बद्दे *badde*, Anyone (feminine) anything.	

	Singular.	Plural.
Genitive,	बदेनोर *badenor*, बदेना *badená*.	
Dat. & Acc.	बदेने *badene*.	
Locative,	बवेटे *baweṭe*.	Unused.
Ablative,	बदेनसे *badense*.	
Prep. root,	बदेने *badene*.	

Undeclinable :—सबही *sabhí*, every.
अमुहच *amuhach*, a few.
वल्ले *walle*, many.
बारइ *bárai*, something.

Interrogative Pronouns.

	Singular.	Plural.
Nominative,	बोर *bor*, who? (masculine).	
Genitive,	बोनोर *bonor*, बोनोर्क *bonork*, बोना *boná*, बोनांग *bonáṇg*.	Unused.
Dat. & Acc.	बोन *bon*.	
Locative,	बवेटे *baweṭe*.	
Ablative,	बोनाळ *bonál*.	
Prep. root,	बोन *bon*.	

बद *bad*, Who? (feminine) Which? is declined similarly to अद *ad*. बत्ती *batti*, What? (neuter) is only used in the nominative case.

N.B.—Distinction between बत्ती *batti* and बारां *báráṇ* and बाल *bál*, all meaning What?

बत्ती *batti* is used with a noun; ex., बत्ती नाताल वातीड़ *batti nátál wátiṛ*, from what village have you come?

बारां *báráṇ* is used alone as What? or is placed at the beginning of a sentence to make it interrogative; ex., बारां इम्मा इदेन इन्दातोनी *báráṇ immá iden indátoní*, dost thou say this?

बाल *bál* is an accusative case; ex., बाल केकी *bal keki*, what wilt thou do?

Relative Pronouns.

The interrogative pronoun बोर *bor* supplies the want of a relative pronoun, and the demonstrative स्रोर *or* that of a correlative; ex., बोरुन ईहुने कीनाके पन्नीर स्रोर धन्य स्रान्दुर *borun íhune kínáke pannír or dhanya ándur*, he shall be blessed whom he shall find so doing.

N.B.—The Hindi relative pronoun जो *jo* corrupted into जोन *jon* is also in common use.

Adjectives.

The number of adjectives in Gondi is very small, most being supplied in a more or less corrupted form by Hindi. They are not affected by number case or gender; ex., इद बचका पोहटा स्रान्द

id bachká pohtá ánd, this load is heavy; एर्के माड़-सालोर्के वल्ले ढोंगल आन्दुर्के *erk márṣálork walle ḍhoṇgal ándurk,* these men are very tall.

Hindi adjectives, when used, if ending in आ *á* change the आ *á* into ओ *o*; ex., बुरा *burá,* evil, becomes बुरो *buro*; सूना *súná* empty, सूनो *súno.*

Participial adjectives are fairly numerous, ending almost always in आल *ál*; ex., पैहताल *páihatál,* rent; वत्ताल *wattál,* dry; पाहनाल *páhnál,* wet.

Comparison of adjectives is formed by the addition of उड़े *uṛe* for the comparative, and सबताल *sabtál* or सबसे *sabse* for the superlative; ex., संघरो *saṇghro,* dense; उड़े संघरो *uṛe saṇghro,* more dense; सबताल संघरो *sabtál saṇghro,* most dense.

Numerals.

The Gond language only possesses numerals of its own up to ten; if it originally had more, no trace of them is anywhere to be found. Above ten the Hindi equivalents are used. In the Mandla, Jubbulpore, and Balaghat Districts, for which alone I can speak, the Gondi forms for eight and nine have also become obsolete, but I give them below on the authority of the Rev. J. Dawson's vocabulary in the *Journal of the Asiatic Society of Bengal.*

उन्दी *undí*, one.	सारुंग *sárúṇg*, six.
रण्ड *raṇḍ*, two.	येड़ुंग *yeṛúṇg*, seven.
मूण्ड *múṇḍ*, three.	अर्मुर *armur*, eight.
नालुंग *nálúṇg*, four.	उन्माक *unmák*, nine.
सैयुंग *sáiyúṇg*, five.	पद *pad*, ten.

The Gondi numerals रण्ड *raṇḍ* and मूण्ड *múṇḍ* when used as plural substantives are declined; ex. रंटेनोर *raṇṭenor* or रण्डेनोर *raṇḍenor*, of the two; मुंटेनुंग *múṇṭenúṇg*, the three.

THE VERB.

The Gond Verb is well supplied with Moods and Tenses.

Of Moods, it possesses indicative, subjunctive, potential, inceptive, imperative, and infinitive, besides participles past and present.

Of Tenses, it possesses present, perfect, pluperfect, imperfect, past, future, paulo-post future, and indefinite imperfect.

The conjugation of the verb कीआना *kíáná* is given below in full.

The Verb कीआना *kíáná,* to do (Hindi करना).

Root की *kí.*

INDICATIVE MOOD.

Present Tense (H. मैं करता हूं).

	Singular.	Plural.
1st per.	नन्ना कीआतोना *nanná kíátoná*	मम्माट कीआतोरम *mammáṭ kíátoram*
2nd per.	इम्मा कीआतोनी *immá kíátoní*	इम्माट कीआतोरीट * *immáṭ kíátoríṭ*
3rd per. masc.	ओर कीआतोर *or kíátor*	ओर्क कीआतोर्क *ork kíátork.*
3rd per. fem. or neut.	अद कीआता *ad kíátá*	औ कीआतांग *áú kíátáṇg*

Perfect Tense (H. मैंने किया है).

	Singular.	Plural.
1st per.	नन्ना कीतोना *nanná kítoná*	मम्माट कीतोरम *mammáṭ kítoram.*
2nd per.	इम्मा कीतोनी *immá kítoní*	इम्माट कीतोरीट * *immáṭ kítoríṭ.*
3rd per. masc.	ओर कीतोर *or kítor*	ओर्क कीतोर्क *ork kítork.*
3rd per. fem. or neut.	अद, कीता *ad kítá*	औ कीतांग *áú kítáṇg.*

* The final ट *ṭ* of the 2nd person plural very commonly becomes ड़ *ṛ*.

Pluperfect Tense (मैंने किया था).

	Singular.	Plural.
1st per.	नन्ना कीसी मत्तोना *nanná kísí mattoná.*	मम्माट कीसी मत्तोरम *mammáṭ kísí mattoram.*
2nd per.	इम्मा कीसी मत्तोनी *immá kísí mattoní.*	इम्माट कीसी मत्तोरीट* *immáṭ kísí mattoríṭ.*
3rd per. masc.	ओर कीसी मत्तोर *or kísí mattor.*	ओर्क कीसी मत्तोर्क *ork kísí mattork.*
3rd per. fem. or neut.	अद कीसी मत्ता *ad kísí mattá.*	औ कीसी मत्तांग *áú kísí mattáṇg.*

Imperfect Tense (H. मैं करता था).

	Singular.	Plural.
1st per.	नन्ना कीन्दान *nanná kíndán.*	मम्माट कीन्दोम *mammáṭ kíndom.*
2nd per.	इम्मा कीन्दी *immá kíndí.*	इम्माट कीन्दीट* *immáṭ kíndíṭ.*
3rd per. masc.	ओर कीन्दुर *or kíndur.*	ओर्क कीन्दुर्क *ork kíndurk.*
3rd per. fem. or neut.	अद कीन्द *ad kínd.*	औ कीन्दुंग *áú kínduṇg.*

* The final ट *ṭ* of the 2nd person plural very commonly becomes ड़ *ṛ*.

Past Tense (H. मैंने किया).

	Singular.	Plural.
1st per.	नन्ना कीतान *nanná kitán.*	मम्माट कीतोम *mammáṭ kítom.*
2nd per.	इम्मा कीती *immá kití.*	इम्माट कीतीड़ *immáṭ kitíṛ.*
3rd per. masc.	ओर कीतुर *or kítur.*	ओर्क कीतुर्क *ork kíturk.*
3rd per. fem. or neut.	अद कीत *ad kít.*	औ कीतुंग *áú kituṇg.*

Future Tense (H. मैं करूंगा).

	Singular.	Plural.
1st per.	नन्ना कीआका* *nanná kiáká.*	मम्माट कीआकोम *mammáṭ kiákom.*
2nd per.	इम्मा कीआकी *immá kiákí.*	इम्माट कीआकीड़ *immáṭ kiákíṛ.*
3rd per. masc.	ओर कीआनुर *or kiánur.*	ओर्क कीआनुर्क *ork kiánurk.*
3rd per. fem. or neut.	अद कीआर *ad kiár.*	औ कीआनुंग *áú kiánuṇg.*

* Commonly contracted into केका *kéká,* केकी *keki,* कानुर *káṇur,* &c.

Paulo-Post Future (H. मैं किया होऊंगा).

	Singular.	Plural.
1st per.	नन्ना कीसी मन्दाका *nanná kísí mandáká.*	मम्माट कीसी मन्दाकोम *mammáṭ kísí-mandákom.*
2nd per.	इम्मा कीसी मन्दाकी *immá kísí mandákí.*	इम्माट कीसी मन्दाकीट* *immáṭ kísí mandákíṭ.*
3rd per. masc.	ओर कीसी मन्दानुर *or kísí mandánur.*	ओर्क कीसी मन्दानुर्क *ork kísí mandánurk*
3rd per. fem. or neut.	अद कीसी मन्दार *ad kísí mandár.*	औ कीसी मन्दानुंग *áú kísí mandánuṇg*

Indefinite Imperfect (H. मैं करता).

	Singular.	Plural.
1st per.	नन्ना कीएना *nanná kiená.*	मम्माट कीएरोम *mammáṭ kierom.*
2nd per.	इम्मा कीएनी *immá kiení.*	इम्माट कीएरीट* *immáṭ kieríṭ.*
3rd per. masc.	ओर कीएर *or kíer.*	ओर्क कीएर्क *ork kíerk.*
3rd per. fem. or neut.	अद कीवार *ad kíwár.*	औ कीवांग *áú kíwáṇg.*

* The final ट *ṭ* of the 2nd person plural very commonly becomes ड़ *ṛ*.

SUBJUNCTIVE MOOD.

Present Tense (H. मैं करूं).

	Singular.	Plural.
1st per.	नन्ना कीआका *nanná kiáká.*	मम्माट कीआकोम *mammáṭ kiákom.*
2nd per.	इम्मा कीआकी *immá kiáki.*	इम्माट कीआकीट * *immáṭ kiákit.*
3rd per. masc.	ओर कीर *or kir.*	ओर्क कीर्क *ork kirk.*
3rd per. fem. or neut.	अद की *ad ki.*	औ कींग *áú kiṇg.*

IMPERATIVE MOOD.

(H. कर करो.)

	Singular.	Plural.
2nd per.	कीम *kim.*	कीम्ट *kimṭ.*

INFINITIVE MOOD.

(H. करना करनेको.)

कीआना *kiáná,* कीआले *kiále.*

* The final ट *ṭ* of tho 2nd person plural very commonly becomes ड़ *ṛ*.

PARTICIPLES.

(H. करके.)

कीसी *kísí*, कीसीकुन *kísíkun.*

(H. करते हुए.)

कीतेके *kíteke.*

POTENTIAL.

Present Tense (H. मैं कर सक्ता हूं)

1st per. नन्ना कीआ पड़ीतोना

nanná kíá paṛítoná, &c.

Perfect Tense (H. मैं कर सका हूं).

1st per. नन्ना कीआ पड़तोना

nanná kíá paṛtoná, &c.

Pluperfect Tense (H. मैं कर सका था).

1st per. नन्ना कीआ पड़सी मत्तोना

nanná kíá paṛsí mattoná, &c.

Imperfect Tense (H. मैं कर सक्ता था).

1st per. नन्ना कीआ पड़न्दान

nanná kíá paṛndán, &c.

Past Tense (H. मैं कर सका).

1st per. नन्ना कीश्रा पड़तान

nanná kíá paṛtán, &c.

Future Tense (H. मैं कर सकूंगा).

1st per. नन्ना कीश्रा पड़ाका

nanná kíá paṛáká, &c.

and regularly through the remaining tenses.

INCEPTIVE.

Present Tense (H. मैं करने लगता हूं).

1st per. नन्ना कीश्रा लातोना

nanná kíá látoná, &c.

Imperfect Tense (H. मैं करने लगता था).

1st per. नन्ना कीश्रा लातान

nanná kíá látán, &c.

and regularly through all the tenses.

With the Negative हिल्ले *hille.*

The perfect, imperfect, past, future, and indefinite imperfect tenses of the indicative mood, when coupled with the negative हिल्ले *hille*, are conjugated thus:—

	Singular.	Plural.
1st per.	नन्ना हिल्ले कीओन *nanná hille kíon.*	मम्माट हिल्ले कीओम *mammáṭ hille kíom.*
2nd pers.	इम्मा हिल्ले केवी *immá hille kewí.*	इम्माट हिल्ले केवीड़ *immáṭ hille kewíṛ.*
3rd per. masc.	ओर हिल्ले कीओर *or hille kíor.*	ओर्क हिल्ले कीओर्क *ork hille kíork.*
3rd per. fem. or neut.	अद हिल्ले कीओ *ad hille kío.*	औ हिल्ले कीओं *áú hille kíoṇ.*

The context will usually determine which of the above tenses is being used, for example :— इम्मा कीतोनी कि हिल्ले केवी *immá kítoní ki hille kewí,* Hast thou done it or not done it.

The pluperfect tense with the negative is conjugated as follows :—

	Singular.
1st per.	नन्ना हिल्ले केवाके *nanná hille kewáke.*
2nd per.	इम्मा हिल्ले केवाके *immá hille kewáke.*

and so throughout the singular and plural.

The only other parts of the verb affected by the addition of the negative are the second persons singular and plural of the imperative mood, which, with मिन्ने *minne,* do not, become केमा *kemá* and केमाट *kemáṭ* or केमाड़ *kemáṛ.*

N.B.—The present tense of this verb कीश्राना *kíáná,* often appears as कीश्राल्तोना *kíáltoná* and काल्तोना *káltoná,* कीश्राल्तोनी *kíáltoní,* &c.

Conjugation of the verbs श्रायाना *áyáná,* and मन्दाना *mandáná,* both signifying 'to be,' the latter with the sense of 'remaining' or 'continuing to be.'

Verb श्रायाना *áyáná,* 'to be' (H. होना).

Root श्रा *á.*

PARTICIPLES.

श्रासी *ásí,* श्रासीकुन *ásíkun,* श्रासोके *ásoke.*

INDICATIVE MOOD.

Present Tense (H. होता हूं).

श्रायातोना *áyátoná,* or

(H. हो जाता हूं).

श्रासी हन्दातोना *ásí handátoná.*

Imperfect Tense (H. होता था or हूं),

(generally used as a Present Tense).

श्रान्दान *ándán.*

Perfect Tense (H. हुश्रा हूं).

श्रातोना *átoná.*

Pluperfect Tense (H. हुआ था).

आसी मत्तोना *ásí mattoná.*

Past Tense (H. हुआ).

आतान *átán.*

Future Tense (H. हुंगा).

आयाका *áyáká.*

Paulo-Post Future Tense (H. हो जाऊंगा).

आसी हन्दाका *ásí handáká.*

Indefinite Imperfect Tense (H. होता).

आयेना *áyená.*

IMPERATIVE MOOD.

(H. हो.)

आम *ám.*

POTENTIAL MOOD.

(H. हो सक्ता).

आया पड़ीतोना *áyá paṛitoná.*

INCEPTIVE MOOD.

(H. होने लगता हूं).

आया लातोना *áyá látoná.*

Verb मन्दाना *mandáná*, 'to be,' or 'to remain.'

(H. रहना). Root मन *man*.

PARTICIPLES.

मंजी *manjí*, मंजीकुन *manjíkun*.

INDICATIVE MOOD.

Present Tense (H. हूं). मन्दोना *mandoná*, or

(H. रहता हूं). मन्दातोना *mandátoná*.

Perfect Tense (H. रहा हूं). मत्तोना *mattoná*.

Pluperfect Tense (H. रहा था).

मंजी मत्तोना *manjí mattoná*.

Imperfect Tense (H. रहता था). मन्दान *mandan*.

Past Tense (H. रहा). मंजी हत्तान *manjí hattán*.

Future Tense (H. रहूंगा). मन्दाका *mandáká*.

Paulo-Post Future Tense (H. रह जाऊंगा).

मंजी हन्दाका *manjí handáká*.

Indefinite Imperfect Tense (H. रहता).

मन्नेना *mannená*.

IMPERATIVE MOOD.

(H. रह).

मन *man*.

POTENTIAL MOOD.

(H. रह सक्ता).

मन्दा पड़ीतोना *mandá paṛitoná.*

INCEPTIVE MOOD.

(H. रहने लगता हूं).

मन्दा लातोना *mandá látoná.*

Negative tenses of आयाना *áyáná* are आयोन *áyon* and आवाके *áwáke;* of मन्दाना *mandáná* are मन्नोन *mannon* and मन्नाके *mannáke;* and the imperative with मिन्ने becomes आयिमा *áyimá* and मनमा *manmá.*

Two notes with regard to the Imperative.

(1) The negative form of the imperative does not necessarily require the मिन्ने *minne* to be expressed:—as, for ex., ईहुने केमाड़ *íhune kemáṛ,* Don't do so.

(2) In some few verbs an alternative form of the imperative is prefered, ending in उम *um*:—as, for ex., from तत्ताना *tattáná* तच्छुम *tachchhum,* from तन्दाना *tandáná,* तंड़सुम *taṇṛsum;* from नच्चाना *nachcháná,* नच्छुम *nachchhum;* from वहताना, *wahtáná,* वहचुम *wahchum.*

PARADIGM OF THE VERB सीश्राना *síáná*, 'to give.'

TENSE.	INDICATIVE MOOD.						
	Without Negative.				With Negative.		
		1st Per.	2nd Per.	3rd Per.	1st Per.	2nd Per.	3rd Per.
Present	सीश्रात *síát*				सीश्रोन *síon*	सेवी *sewí*	सीश्रोर सीश्रो *síor sío*
Perfect	सीत *sít*	श्रोना *oná*	श्रोनी *oní*	श्रोर श्रा *or á*	सीश्रोम *síom*	सेवीड़ *sewíṛ*	सीश्रोर्क सीनों *síork síoṇ*
Pluperfect	सीसी मत्त *sísí matt*	श्रोरम *oram*	श्रोरीट *oríṭ*	श्रोर्क श्रांग *ork áṅg*	सेवाके *sewáke*		
Imperfect	सीन्द *sínd*	श्रान *án*	ई *í*	उर उ *ur u*			
Past	सीत *sít*	श्रोम *om*	ईट *íṭ*	उर्क उंग *urk uṅg*			
Future	सीश्रा *síá*	का *ká*	की *kí*	नुर र *nur r*	all	like the	present.
Paulo-Post Future	सीसी मन्दा *sísí mandá*	कोम *kom*	कीट *kíṭ*	नुर्क नुंग *nurk nuṅg*			
Indef. Imp.	सी *sí*	एना *ená*	एनी *ení*	एर वार *er wár*			
		एरोम *erom*	एरीट *eríṭ*	एर्क वांग *erk wáṅg*			

TENSE.	SUBJUNCTIVE MOOD.				POTENTIAL MOOD.		INCEPTIVE MOOD.		IMPERATIVE MOOD. Without Negative.		IMPERATIVE MOOD. With Negative.	
		1st Per.	2nd Per.	3rd Per.		1st Per.		1st Per.	2 Per. Sing.	2 Per. Plu.	2 Per. Sing.	2 Per. Plu.
Present	सी *sí*	आका *áká*	आकी *ákí*	र — *r* -	सीआ *síá*	पड़ीतोना *paṛítoná*	सीआ *síá*	लातोना *látoná*	* सीम *sím*	* सीम्ट *símṭ*	सेमा *semá*	सेमाट *semáṭ*
Perfect		आकोम *ákom*	आकीट *ákíṭ*	र्क ंग *rk ng*	,,	पड़तोना *paṛtoná*						
Pluperfect					,,	पड़सी मत्तोना *paṛsí mattoná*						
Imperfect ...					,,	पड़न्दान *paṛndán*						
Past					,,	पड़तान *paṛtán*	,,	लातान *látán*				
Future					,,	पड़ाका *paṛáká*						
Paulo-Post Future					,,	पड़सी मन्दाका *paṛsí mandáká*						
Indef. Imp.					,,	पड़ेना *paṛená*						

* Or सीसुम *sísum*, सीसुम्ट *sísumṭ*.

Paradigm of fifteen Verbs in common use.

Infinitive.	Pres. Indic.	Perf. Indic.	Pluperfect.	Imperfect.	Past.	Future.
कीआना to do .... *kíáná*	कीआतोना *kíátoná*	कीतोना *kítoná*	कीसी मत्तोना *kísí mattoná*	कीन्दान *kíndán*	कीतान *kítán*	कीआका *kíáká*
हन्दाना to go......... *handáná*	हन्दातोना *handátoná*	हत्तोना *hattoná*	हंजी मत्तोना *hanjí mattoná*	हत्तान *hattán*	हत्तान *hattán*	हन्दाका *handáká*
ताकाना to walk .... *tákáná*	ताकीतोना *tákítoná*	ताक्तोना *táktoná*	ताक्सी मत्तोना *táksí mattoná*	ताकन्दान *tákandán*	ताक्तान *táktán*	ताकीका *tákíká*
इर्राना to put .... *irráná*	इर्रातोना *irrátoná*	इर्तोना *irtoná*	इर्सी मत्तोना *irsí mattoná*	इरन्दान *irandán*	इर्तान *irtán*	इर्राका *irráká*
तेदाना to rise......... *tedáná*	तेदातोना *tedátoná*	तेद्तोना *tedtoná*	तेच्छी मत्तोना *techchhí mattoná*	तेद्दान *teddán*	तेतान *tetán*	तेदाका *tedáká*
तरगाना to ascend... *targáná*	तरगीतोना *targítoná*	तर्गतोना *targtoná*	तर्गसी मत्तोना *targsí mattoná*	तरंगदान *taruṇ idán*	तर्गतान *targtán*	तरगीका *targíká*
वायाना to come .... *wáyáná*	वाइतोना *wáitoná*	वातोना *wátoná*	वासी मत्तोना *wásí mattoná*	वान्दान *wándán*	वात्तान *wáttán*	वाइका *wáiká*
तत्ताना to bring .... *tattáná*	तत्तातोना *tattátoná*	तत्तोना *tattoná*	तच्छी मत्तोना *tachchhí mattoná*	तरन्दान *tarandán*	तत्तान *tattán*	तत्ताका* *tattáká*

* Or तत्तका *tattká.*

Infinitive.	Pres. Indic.	Perf. Indic.	Pluperfect.	Imperfect.	Past.	Future.
उद्दीना to sit .... *uddíná*	उद्दीतोना *uddítoná*	उद्दतोना *uddtoná*	उच्छी मत्तोना *uchchhí mattoná*	उद्दन्दान *uddandán*	उत्तान *uttán*	उद्दीका *uddíká*
तेहताना to raise .... *tehtáná*	तेहतातोना *tehtátoná*	तेहतोना *tehtoná*	तेहची मत्तोना *tehchí mattoná*	तेहन्दान *tehandán*	तेहतान *tehtán*	तेहताका *tehtáká*
तिन्दाना to eat........ *tindáná*	तिन्दातोना *tindátoná*	तित्तोना *tittoná*	तिंजी मत्तोना *tinjí mattoná*	तिन्दान *tindán*	तित्तान *tittán*	तिन्दाका *tindáká*
उन्दाना to drink........ *undáná*	उन्दातोना *undátoná*	उत्तोना *uttoná*	उंजी मत्तोना *unjí mattoná*	उत्तन्दान *uttandán*	उत्तान *uttán*	उन्दाका *undáká*
मन्दाना to be .... *mandáná*	मन्दातोना *mandátoná*	मत्तोना *mattoná*	————	मन्दान *mandán*	मत्तान *mattán*	मन्दाका *mandáká*
केंजाना to hear........ *kenjáná*	केंजीतोना *kenjítoná*	केंजतोना *kenjtoná*	केंची मत्तोना *kenchí mattoná*	केंजन्दान *kenjandán*	केंजतान *kenjtán*	केंजीका *kenjíká*
रोमीना to rest........ *romíná*	रोमीतोना *romítoná*	रोम्तोना *romtoná*	रोम्सी मत्तोना *romsí mattoná*	रोमदान *romdán*	रोमतान *romtán*	रोमीका *romíká*

N.B.—Supines are formed by adding आले *ále* to the root, as कीआले *kíále*, हन्दाले *handále*, ताकाले *tákále*, &c.

PARADIGM OF FIFTEEN VERBS IN COMMON USE (*continued*).

Infinitive.	Negative.	Pres. Part.	Imperative.	Subj.	Potential.	Inceptive.
कीआना to do ...... *kíáná*	कीओन *kíon*	कीतेके *kíteke*	कीम *kím*	कीएना *kíená*	कीआ पड़ीतोना *kíá paṛítoná*	कीआ लातोना *kíá látoná*
हन्दाना to go ...... *handáná*	हनोन *hanon*	हत्तेके *hatteke*	हन *han*	हन्नेना *hannená*	हन्दा पड़ीतोना *handá paṛítoná*	हन्दा लातोना *handá látoná*
ताकाना to walk ...... *tákáná*	ताकोन *tákon*	ताक्केके *tákteke*	ताका *táká*	ताकेना *tákená*	ताकी पड़ीतोना *tákí paṛítoná*	ताकी लातोना *tákí látoná*
इर्राना to put ...... *irráná*	इर्रोन *irron*	इर्तेके *irteke*	इर्रा *irrá*	इर्रेना *irrená*	इर्रा पड़ीतोना *irrá paṛítoná*	इर्रा लातोना *irrá látoná*
तेदाना, to rise ...... *tedáná*	तेदोन *tedon*	तेदतेके *tedteke*	तेदा *tedá*	तेदेना *tedená*	तेदा पड़ीतोना *tedá paṛítoná*	तेदा लातोना *tedá látoná*
तरगाना to ascend ... *targáná*	तरगोन *targon*	तर्गतेके *targteke*	तरगा *targá*	तरगेना *targená*	तरगी पड़ीतोना *targí paṛítoná*	तरगी लातोना *targí látoná*
वायाना to come ...... *wáyáná*	वायोन *wáyon*	वातेके *wáteke*	वरा *wará*	वाएना *wáená*	वाया पड़ीतोना *wáyá paṛítoná*	वाया लातोना *wáyá látoná*
तत्ताना to bring ...... *tattáná*	तत्तोन *tatton*	तत्तेके *tatteke*	तरा *tará*	तरेना *tarená*	तत्ता पड़ीतोना *tattá paṛítoná*	तत्ता लातोना *tattá látoná*

Infinitive.	Negative.	Pres. Part.	Imperative.	Subj.	Potential.	Inceptive.
उद्दीना to sit .... *uddíná*	उद्दोन *uddon*	उत्तेके *utteke*	उद्दा *uddá*	उद्देना *uddená*	उद्दी पड़ीतोना *uddí paṛítoná*	उद्दी लातोना *uddí látoná*
तेहताना to raise .... *tehtáná*	तेहोन *tehon*	तेहतेके *tehteke*	तेहा *tehá*	तेहेना *tehená*	तेहता पड़ीतोना *tehtá paṛítoná*	तेहता लातोना *tehtá látoná*
तिन्दाना to eat............ *tindáná*	तिनोन *tinon*	तित्तेके *titteke*	तिन *tin*	तिनेना *tinená*	तिन्दा पड़ीतोना *tindá paṛítoná*	तिन्दा लातोना *tindá látoná*
उन्दाना to drink......... *undáná*	उन्नोन *unnon*	उत्तेके * *utteke*	उन *un*	उन्नेना *unnená*	उन्दा पड़ीतोना *undá paṛítoná*	उन्दा लातोना *undá látoná*
मन्दाना to be .... *mandáná*	मनोन *manon*	मत्तेके *matteke*	मन *man*	मन्नेना *mannená*	मन्दा पड़ीतोना *mandá paṛítoná*	मन्दा लातोना *mandá látoná*
केंजाना to hear............ *kenjáná*	केंजोन *kenjon*	केंजतेके *kenjteke*	केंजा *kenjá*	केंजेना *kenjená*	केंजी पड़ीतोना *kenjí paṛítoná*	केंजी लातोना *kenjí látoná*
रोमीना to rest............ *romíná*	रोमोन *romon*	रोमतेके *romteke*	रोमा *romá*	रोमेना *romená*	रोमी पड़ीतोना *romí paṛítoná*	रोमी लातोना *romí látoná*

N.B.—Supines are formed by adding आले *ále* to the root, as कीआले *kiále*, हन्दाले *handále*, ताकाले *tákále*, &c.

* Or उन्देके *undeke.*

Adverbs.

Of place.

बग्गा *baggá*, where?
अग्गा *aggá*, there.
इग्गा *iggá*, here.
उड़े बग्गने *uṛe baggane*, elsewhere.
रोपा *ropá*, within.
बाहरो *báharo*, outside.
मुन्ने *munne*, before.
पिज्जा *pijjá*, behind.
पर्रो *parro*, above.
सिरी *sirí*, beneath.
बग्गाटाल *baggáṭál* or बग्गाहड़ा *baggáhaṛá*, whence?
अग्गाटाल *aggáṭál* or अग्गाहड़ा *aggáhaṛá*, thence.
इग्गाटाल *iggáṭál* or इग्गाहड़ा *iggáhaṛá*, hence.
लक *lak*, far.
पुरीत *purít*, near.
बिक्के टाल *bikke ṭál*, which way?
हिक्के टाल *hikke ṭál*, this way.

Of time.

बप्पोर *bappor*, when?
नेड़ *neṛ*, to-day.
इंगा *ingá*, now.
इन्देके *indeke*, now (*emphatically*).
नाड़ी *náṛí*, yesterday.
नर्काई *narkaí*, to-morrow.

झेर *jher*, late.
बप्पोरे *bappore*, sometimes.
इंगा टाल *ingá ṭál*, henceforth.

Of order, manner, degree, quantity.

बातल *bátal*, how ?
इच्चोरे *ichchore*, so much.
बच्चोरे *bachchore*, how much ?
ईहुने *íhune*, thus.
नक्का *nakká*, more, or much.

Of affirmation and negation.

इंगे *iṇge*, yes.
हिल्ले *hille*, no, not.

N.B.—The rest are supplied from Hindi.

PREPOSITIONS.

The only true preposition is the word बिगुड़ *biguṛ*, except, adopted from Hindi.

Postpositions :—पिज्जा *pijjá*, after; नडुम *naḍum*, between; हिक्के *hikke*, towards; लाने *láne*, for (corrupted Hindi); सिरी *sirí*, under; परों *parro*, upon; लग *lag*, as far as (Hindi).

Suffixes :—ते *te*, at, in; टाल *ṭál*, or ताल *tál*, from.

CONJUNCTIONS.

Connective :—अनि *ani*, and; सोई *soí*, also (Hindi); बप्पोरे *bappore*, sometimes.

Adversative :—पे *pe*, but.

The Hindi and Urdu words for 'but' are also in common use.

Conclusive :—ईहुन *íhun*, thus; इदेन लाने *iden láne*, therefore.

INTERJECTIONS.

अरे *are*, what! Oh! (Hindi); धर्त *dhart*, be off!

Astonishment is generally expressed by a 'cl'ck' of the tongue.

VOCABULARY.

English.	Gondi.	Hindi.
Abandon, *v.*	पोहताना *pohtáná*, पोहची सीआना *pohchí siáná.*	छोड़ना, छोड़ देना.
Abandoned, *adj.*	पोहताल *pohtál*, नक्का बुरो *nakká buro.*	छोड़ा हुआ, बहुत बुरा.
Abate, *v. i.*	घटे मायाना *ghaṭe máyáná.*	घटना.
Abate, *v. t.*	घटे कीआना *ghaṭe kiáná.*	घटाना.
Abet, *v.*	उभड़े कीआना *ubhaṛe kiáná.*	उभाड़ना.
Abhor, *v.*	घिन्ने मायाना *ghinne máyáná.*	घिन करना.
Abide, *v.*	मन्दाना *mandáná.*	रहना.
Able (strong), *adj.*	नालुंग्वल्क *náluṇg-walk.*	बलवान.
Absorb, *v.*	सोखे कीआना *sokhe kiáná.*	सोखना.
Abundant, *adj.*	नक्का *nakká.*	बहुतसा.
Abuse, *v.*	रांगीना *ráṇginá.*	गाली देना.

English.	Gondi.	Hindi.
Accelerate, *v.*	झप कीसेहताना *jhap kísehtáná.*	जलदी कराना.
Accept, *v.*	येताना *yetáná.*	लेना.
Accumulate, *v.*	वर्पने कीआना *warpne kíáná.*	बटोरना.
Achár tree (*Buchanania latifolia*), *n.*	सड़ेका *saṛeká.*	अचार पेड़.
Ache, *v.*	नोईताना *noítáná.*	दुखना.
Acid, *adj.*	सवीटाल *sawíṭál.*	खट्टा.
Acquire, *v.*	पन्नाना *pannáná,* कैदे कीआना *káide kíáná.*	मिलना, हाथमें करना.
Adjoining, *adj.*	सटे मातल *saṭe mátal.*	लगा हुआ.
Admit (allow entrance to), *v.*	नेंगी सीआना *neṅgí siáná.*	पैठने देना.
Advance, *v.*	वीड़ाना *wíṛáná.*	आगे आना.
Adze, *n.*	टट्टी *ṭaṭṭí.*	बसूला.
Affright, *v.*	वर्रहताना *warrahtáná.*	डराना.
After, *prep.*	पिजा *pijá.*	पीछे.
Afterwards, *adv.*	इदेना पिजा *idená pijá.*	इस के पीछे.
Again, *adv.*	उड़े *uṛe,* इस्सुर *issur,* घरीक्सी *gharíksí.*	फिर, दूसरी बार, थोड़ी देर में.
Aged, *adj.*	सेनाल *senál,* सेनो *seno.*	बूढ़ा, बूढ़ी.

English.	Gondi.	Hindi.
Agree, *v.*	एक मन आयाना *ek man áyáná.*	एक मन होना.
Ailing, *p. part.*	बिजार *bijár.*	बीमार.
Air, *n.*	वरी *warí.*	हवा.
Alive, *adj.*	पिस्ताल *pistál.*	जीता.
All, *pron.*	सब *sab.*	सब.
Alone, *adj.*	वरोर *waror.*	अकेला.
Aloud, *adv.*	किलीसी *kilísí.*	पुकारके.
Also, *adv.*	सोई *soí.*	भी.
Among, *prep.*	नडुम *nadum.*	बीच.
Ancestors, *n.*	पुरखाल्क *purkhálk.*	पुरखे.
Ancient, *adj.*	जूनाल *júnál.*	पुराना.
Ancle, *n.*	हूराकाल *húrákál.*	टकना.
And, *conj.*	अनि *ani.*	और.
Anger, *n.*	सोंगा *soṇgá.*	क्रोध.
Ant, *n.*	पत्ते *patte.*	चिऊंटी.
—— large	घोघाल *ghogál.*	चिऊंटा.
—— red	शरवटले *sharwaṭle.*	लाल चिऊंटी.
—— white	अल्लुम *allum.*	दीमक.
Any, *pron.*	बोरे *bore,* बद्दे *badde,* बत्ती *battí,* बारअई *[bárai.*	कोई, कुछ.
Aonla tree (*Phillanthus emblica*), *n.*	नल्ली *nallí.*	आंवला.
Ape, *n.*	मूंजाल *múṇjál,* रटुआ *[raṭuá.*	बन्दर.
—— black, *n.*	ढडुआ *ḍhaṛuá.*	काला बन्दर.

English.	Gondi.	Hindi.
Apparel, *n.*	दिकड़ी *dikṛí.*	कपड़ा.
Appear, *v.*	दीसाना *dísáná.*	देख पड़ना.
Apply, *v.*	लागसहताना *lágsahtáná.*	लगाना.
Archer, *n.*	कमटा कीआनवारे. *kamṭá kíánwáre.*	कमठैत.
Arise, *v.*	टेदाना *ṭedáná.*	उठना.
Arm-pit, *n.*	ककरी *kakrí.*	कखरी.
Army, *n.*	पेनढारी *penḍhárí.*	सेना.
Around, *prep.*	नालुंगे पट्टी *nálungepaṭṭí.*	चारों ओर.
Arouse, *v.*	टेहताना *ṭehtáná*	उठाना.
Arrive, *v.*	अव्वाना *awwáná*	पहुंचना.
As, *conj.*	बाहुन *báhun,* लेका *leká.*	जैसा, समान.
Ascend, *v.*	तरगाना *targáná*	चढ़ना,
Ashes, *n.*	नीर *nír.*	राख.
Ask, *v.*	पूच्छे कीआना *puchchhe kíáná.*	पूछना.
Asleep, *v.*	सुंजताल *sunjtál.*	सोता हुआ.
Ass, *n.*	गधाल *gadhál.*	गधा.
Assemble, *v. t.*	सकले या सकड़े कीआना *sakle yá sakṛe kíáná.*	इकट्टा करना.
Astray, *adv.*	मारंगताल *márangtál* रचताल *rachtál.*	भूला हुआ, खोया.

English.	Gondi.	Hindi.
At, *prep.*	-ते *-te.* [*tál.*	में.
Athirst, *adv.*	येत्क अस्ताल *yetk as-*	पियासा.
Attire, *v.*	पोंड़सहताना *poṇṛ-sahtáná.*	कपड़े पहिनाना.
Await, *v.*	पोसाना *posáná.*	मार्ग देखना, जोहना.
Awake, *v. i.*	चैले मायाना *cháile máyáná.*	जगाना.
Axe, *n.*	मर्स *mars,* टंगिया *ṭaṇgiyá.*	कुल्हाड़ी.
—(for defence)	तबिली *tabilí.*	फरसा.
Baby, *n.*	छौवा *chhouwá.*	छोता लड़का, छोटी लड़की.
Back, *n.*	मुर्चुल *murchul.*	पीठ.
Backbone, *n*	रिघड़ी *righaṛí.*	रीढ़.
Bag, *n.*	बटुआ *baṭuá.*	बटुआ, थैली.
Bake, *v.*	सुर्राना *surráná.*	सेंकना, पकाना.
Balance, *n.*	तखड़ी *takhaṛí.*	तौलने का कांटा.
Bale, *v.*	रोस्कीना *roskíná,* ओंजे कीआना *onje kíáná.*	उलचना.
Bamboo, *n.*	वड्डुर *waddur.*	बांस.
—— (split up)	पहकी *pahkí.*	चीरा हुआ बांस.
Bank, *n.*	दल्ली *dallí,* खाटी *khá-ṭí,* मोंगा *moṇgá.*	बांध, ढांग, ढेर.
Bar, *v.*	मूछाना *múchháná.*	बन्ध करना.

English.	Gondi.	Hindi.
Baṛ tree (*Ficus Indica*), *n.*	बेरेली *berelí.*	बड़ पेड़.
Barbati (*Samara robusta*), *n.*	चनअई *chanaí.*	बरबत्ती.
Bark (of a tree), [*n.*	तोल *tol.*	छाल, बकला.
Bark, *v.*	मुहचीना *muhchíná.*	भूंकना.
Barren, *adj.*	बंजवाल *baṇjwál.*	बांझ.
Basket, *n.*	सिकोसी *sikosí.*	टोकरी.
Bat, *n.*	चूचूं *chúchúṇ.*	चमगीदड़.
Bathe, *v.*	सपरे कीआना *sapre kíáná.*	नहाना.
Be, *v.*	आयाना *áyáná,* मन्दाना *mandáná.*	होना, रहना.
Bead, *n.*	पन्ने *panne,* पोथी *pothí.*	दाना, गुरिया.
Bean, *n.*	जाटा *jáṭá.*	सेम.
Bear (give birth to), *v.*	वातीना *wátíná,* नत्ताना *nattáná.*	जनना.
—— fruit	सादाना *sádáná.*	फलना.
—— *n.*	अड़जाल *aṛjál.*	भालू.
Beard, *n.*	डाड़वा *ḍáṛwá.*	दाढ़ी.
Beat, *v.*	जीआना *jíáná.*	मारना.
Beauty, *n.*	निक्का *nikká.*	सुन्दरता.
Because, *conj.*	बारीकि *báríki,* इद्देन लाने *idden láne.*	क्योंकि, इस लिये.
Become, *v.*	आसी हन्दाना *ásí handáná.*	हो जाना.

English.	Gondi.	Hindi.
Bed, *n.*	कटुल *kaṭul.*	चारपाई, खटिया.
Bee, *n.*	फूकी वीसी *phúkí wísí,* कानाल वीसी *kánál wísí*	मधु माखी.
Beetle, *n.*	भंगड़ा *bhúṇgṛá.*	गुब्रीला.
Before, *prep.*	मुन्ने *munne.*	पहिले, सामने.
Beg, *v.*	तलह्काना *talaȟ-káná.*	मांगना.
Begin, *v.*	महथुर येताना *mah-thur yetáná.*	आरंभ करना.
—— *incept. v.*	लातोना *látoná.*	लगना.
Behold, *v.*	हूड़ाना *húṛáná.*	देखना.
Bel tree (*Aegle marmelos*), *n.*	माहका *máhká.*	बेल.
Belly, *n.*	पिर *pir.*	पेट.
Below, *prep.*	तरी *tarí,* सिरी *sirí.*	नीचे.
Ber tree (*Zizyphus jujuba*), *n.*	रेंगा *reṇgá.*	बेर.
Besmear, *v.*	उसाना *usáná.*	लीपना.
Best, *adj.*	बेश *besh.*	उत्तम.
Bhiláwa nut (*Semicarpus anacardium*), *n.*	कोहका *kohká.*	भिलावा.
Bhindi (*Hibiscus esculentus*), *n.*	भेड़ा *bheṛá.*	भिंडी.
Big, *adj.*	बड़ोर *baṛor.*	बड़ा.

English.	Gondi.	Hindi.
Bind, *v.*	दोहताना *dohtáná.*	बांधना.
Bird, *n.*	पिट्टे *piṭṭe.*	चिड़िया.
Bit, of bridle, *n.*	करीआरी *kariári.*	ज़ीभी.
Bite, *v.*	कस्काना *kaskáná.*	काट खाना.
Bitter, *adj.*	कईताल *kaitál,* लागले *lágle.*	कड़वा.
Black, *adj.*	कड़िअल *kaṛial.*	काला.
Blame, *v.*	पाप लागसहताना *páp lágsahtáná.*	दोष लगाना.
Blame, *n.*	दोष *dosh,* खोट *khoṭ.*	दोष.
Blanket, *n.*	कमड़ा *kamṛá.*	कम्मल.
Bleed, *v.*	नत्तुर पोंगीना *nattur ponginá.*	लोहू बहना.
Blight, *n.*	झिड़ी *jhiṛí.*	झोला, झिड़ी.
Blind, *adj.*	सूराल *súrál.*	अंधा.
Blood, *n.*	नत्तुर *nattur.*	लोहू.
Blossom, *v.*	पुयाना *puyáná.*	खिलना.
Blow, *v.*	ऊहकाना *úhkáná.*	फूंकना, सुलगाना.
Blunt, *adj.*	बुतले मातल *butle mátal.*	भूतरा, भोंता.
Body, *n.*	मेन्दुल *mendul.*	शरीर.
Bog, *n.*	खान्दो *khándo.*	दलदल, धसन.
Boil, *v. t.*	अटाना *aṭáná.*	उबालना.
—— *v. i.*	ऊसीना *úsíná.*	उबलना.
Bone, *n.*	हाड़ा *háṛá.*	हड्डी, हाड़.
Border, *n.*	सीवा *síwá.*	सीमा.

English.	Gondi.	Hindi.
Borrowed, *p. p.*	टड़तान *ṭaṛtán.*	उधार लिया हुआ.
Bosom, *n.*	कोरा *korá.*	गोदी.
Both, *conj.*	अनि *ani.*	और.
—— *adj. pron.*	रंटे *ranṭe.*	दोनों.
Bough, *n.*	खांदा *khánḍá.* डरिया [*ḍariyá.*	डाली, शाखा.
Bound, *v.*	डहकाना *ḍahkáná.*	कूदना.
Bow, *v.*	मुरसाना *mursáná.*	झुकना.
Bowels, *n.*	पद्दूह *paddúh.*	आंतें.
Boy, *n.*	पेड़गाल *peṛgál.*	लड़का.
Bracelet, *n.*	तन्नोर *tannor,* चूड़ा *chúṛá.*	चूड़ी.
Bread, *n.*	साड़ी *sáṛí.*	रोटी.
Break, *v. i.*	उरूंगाना *urungáná.*	टूटना.
—— *v. t.*	उरेहताना *urehtáná.*	फोड़ना.
Breasts, *n.*	दूदूं *dúdúṇ.*	स्तन.
Bribe, *n.*	लांच *lánch.*	घूस.
Bring, *v.*	तताना *tatáná*	लाना.
Broad, *adj.*	चक्रो *chakro.*	चौड़ा.
Broom, *n.*	कैसार *káisár.*	झाड़.
Brother, *n.*	तम्मुर *tammur.*	भाई.
—— -in-law, *n.*	भाटो *bháṭo.*	बहनोई.
Bruise (grain) *v.*	नोरीताना *noritáná.*	कूटना.
Bucket (of leather), *n.*	पोहरा *pohará.*	डोल, पुरवट.
Buffalo, *n.*	बोदाल *bodál,* अर्मी [*armí.*	बोदा, भैंस.
Bug, *n.*	नर्क *nark.*	खटमल.

English.	Gondi.	Hindi.
Bull, *n.*	सांढाल *sáṇḍhál.*	सांड़.
Bullock, *n.*	कोंडा *koṇḍá,* कुर्रा *kurrá.*	बैल.
—— old	डोबाल *ḍobál.*	बूढ़ा बैल.
Bundle (of wood), *n.*	मौड़ी *mouṛí.*	बोझा, लकड़ी का.
Burden, *n.*	बचका *bachká.*	बोझा, बोझ.
Burial-ground, [*n.*	मरघटी *marghaṭí.*	गाड़ने की जगह.
Burn, *v. i.*	करवाना *karwáná.*	जलना.
—— *v. t.*	मासाना *másáná.*	जलाना.
—— (as a lamp)	बोत्ताना *bottáná.*	बरना.
Burst, *v. i.*	अदसीना *adsíná.*	फूटना.
—— *v. t.*	ओहताना *ohtáná.*	फोड़ना.
Bury, *v.*	मिस्साना *missáná,* गड़सहताना *gaṛsahtáná.*	गाड़ देना.
—— itself (of a thorn)	गड्डीना *gaḍḍíná.*	गड़ जाना.
Business, *n.*	धंधो *dhaṇdho.*	काम.
But, *conj.*	पे *pe.*	परन्तु.
Butter, *n.*	नोना *noná,* नैनू *náinú.*	मक्खन, नैनू.
Butterfly, *n.*	फापे *phápe.*	तितरी.
Buttermilk, *n.*	कुर्रोप *kurrop.*	छाछ.
Buy, *v.*	अस्सीना *assíná.*	मोल लेना.
By (near), *prep.*	मोतिस *motis,* करूम *karrum.*	निकट, पास.

English.	Gondi.	Hindi.
Cackle, *v.*	कटकटे मायाना *kaṭkaṭe máyáná.*	कड़कड़ाना.
Calf, *n.*	पैया *páiyá.*	बछड़ा.
—— (of leg), *n.*	फोतरी *photarí.*	पिंड़ली.
Call, *v.*	केश्राना *keáná.*	बुलाना.
Calve, *v.*	नत्ताना *nattáná.*	ब्याना.
Camel, *n.*	ऊट्टुम *úṭṭum.*	ऊंट.
Camp, *v.*	रैगाना *ráigáná.*	टिकना.
Can, *v.*	पड़कीना *paṛkíná.*	सकना.
Care of (to take), [*v.*	केपाना *kepáná.*	रखाना.
Carriage, *n.*	गाड़ो *gáṛo.*	गाड़ी.
Cast, *v.*	नच्चाना *nachcháná.*	फेंकना.
Cat, *n.*	बीलाल *bílál,* वर्कार *warkár.*	बिल्ली, जंगली बिल्ली.
Catch, *v.*	बैयाना *báiyáná.*	पकड़ना.
Caterpillar, *n.*	भूड़सा पूड़ी *bhúṛsá púṛí.*	झांझा.
Cattle, *n.*	धोर्क *dhork.*	धोर.
Cave, *n.*	खोल *khol.*	खोह.
Certainly, *adv.*	गदने *gadne,* आई न आई *ái na ái.*	सचमुच, हो न हो.
Chaff, *n.*	कुर्मी *kurmí.*	भूसी.
Chain, *n.*	सांकर *sáṇkar.*	सिकड़ी.
Chair, *n.*	कुलसा *kulsá,* मछैया *machháiyá.*	चौकी, मछिया.
Charge (a gun), [*v.*	निहताना *nihtáná.*	भरना.

English.	Gondi.	Hindi.
Cheek, *n.*	कोड़वी *koṛwí.*	गाल.
Chicken, *n.*	चीवाल *chíwál.*	मुर्गी का बच्चा.
Chide, *v.*	डबटे कीआना *ḍabṭe kíáná*, वरेहताना *warehtáná.*	डांटना, डराना.
Child, *n.*	छौवा *chhouwá.*	बच्चा, बालक.
Chirp, *v.*	किल्लीताना *killítáná.*	चहचहाना.
Chisel, *n.*	पोह्पी *pohpí.*	रूखानी.
Choose, *v.*	नबड़े कीआना *nabṛe kíáná.*	चुनना.
Chop, *v.*	नर्काना *narkáná.*	टुकड़ा टुकड़ा करना
Christ, *n.*	ईसा मसीह *Ísá Masíh*	ईसा मसीह.
Cleanse, *v.* [*adj.*	नुर्सी येना *nursí yená.*	धोना, निर्मल करना
Clear (limpid),	छिन्नो *chhinno.*	निर्मल.
Cleave, *v.*	पैयताना *páiyatáná.*	चीरना.
Climb, *v.*	तर्गाना *targáná.*	चढ़ना.
Clothes, *n.*	दिकड़ी *dikṛí.*	कपड़े.
Cloud, *n.*	बादूर *bádúr.*	बादल.
—— (rain), *n.*	पिर्र *pirr.*	मेंह का बादल.
Coat, *n.*	झंगा *jhaṇgá.*	अंगरखा, कुर्ता.
Cock, *n.* [*v.*	घोघोड़ी *ghoghoṛí.*	कुक्कट, मुर्गे.
Cold(to become)	मुरंगाना *muraṇgáná*	ठंढा हो जाना.
Cold, *n.*	पीनी *píní.*	ठंढ.
Collect, *v.*	सिकले कीआना *sikle kíáná.* [*chirní.*	इकट्ठा करना.
Comb, *n.*	गरचा *garchá*, चिरनी	कंघी.

English.	Gondi.	Hindi.
Comb (of cock),	मुकुर *mukur.*	केस.
Come, *v.* [*n.*	वायाना *wáyáná.*	आना.
Compassion, *n.*	कीऊ *kíú.*	दया, करुणा.
Complain, *v.*	ओरहन सीआना *orhan síáná.*	उलहना.
Compound, *a. n.*	वेड़ा *weṛá.*	इहाता.
Comprehend, *v.*	तव्वाना *tawwáná.*	समझना.
Conceal, *v.*	मक्सहताना *maksahtáná,* लुक्सहताना *luksahtáná.*	छिपाना.
Conclude, *v.*	कीसी येताना *kísí yetáná.* [*tál.*	समाप्त करना.
Concubine, *n.*	पाट कीताल *páṭ kí-*	रखी हुई स्त्री.
Contain, *v.*	पोद्दाना *poddáná,* पुर्राना *purráná.*	समाना.
Contributions made daily to village herdsman, *n.*	भांड़ी *bhanṛí.* [*táná.*	अनाज जो पतिदिन अहीर को दिया जाता है.
Convey away, *v.*	अर्री तताना *arrí ta-*	ले जाना.
Cook, *v.*	अटाना *aṭáná.*	पकाना.
Cool, *adj.*	मुरूंगताल *murungtál.*	ठंडा.
Cord, *n.*	नोने *none.*	रस्सी.
Cork, *n.*	ठेनी *ṭhení.*	दट्टा
Corn-mill, *n.*	जत्ता *jattá.*	चक्की.

English.	Gondi.	Hindi.
Cottage, *n.*	टोपड़िया *ṭopaṛiyá.*	झोंपड़ी.
Cotton, *n.*	कपसा *kapsá.*	कपास.
Cough, *n.*	खोकी *khokí*	खांसी, खोखी.
Cough, *v.*	काह्चीना *káhchíná.*	खांसना.
Count, *v.*	लक्काना *lakkáná.*	गिनना.
Courtyard, *n.*	रचा *rachá.*	आंगन.
Cover, *v.*	मुड़ताना *muṛutáná.*	ढांपना.
Cover, *n.*	मुँछे *muchchhe.*	ढकनी.
Cow, *n.*	मड़ा *maṛá*, टाली [*ṭálí.*	गाय.
—— (till it has calved), *n.*	पड्डा *paḍḍá.*	गाया.
Cow-pat, *n.*	चेना *chená.*	कण्डा.
Cowshed, *n.*	कोड़का *koṛká.*	गोशाला.
Crab, *n.*	येटे *yeṭe.*	केकड़ा.
Cradle, *n.*	उखाड़ी *ukháṛí.*	हिंडोला.
Crave, *v.*	पड़कीना *paṛkíná.*	चाहना.
Crawl, *v.*	कोड़िताना *koṛitáná.*	रेंगना.
Creeper, *n.*	जल्ली *jallí.*	बेलि.
Crocodile, *n.*	मुगड़ाल *mugṛál.*	मगर.
Crooked, *adj.*	बाकड़ाल *bákṛál.*	टेढ़ा.
Crow, *n.*	कावाल *káwál.*	कौवा.
Crow, *v.*	खूसाना *khúsáná.*	बांग देना.
Cruel, *adj.*	निठुर *niṭhur.*	निर्दय.
Cry out, *v.*	किल्लीताना *killítáná.*	चिल्लाना.
Cubit, *n.*	कूटा *kúṭá.*	हाथ भर माप.

English.	Gondi.	Hindi.
Cucumber, *n.*	अह्कूम *ahkúm.*	खीरा, ककरी.
Curse, *v.*	कोसे कीआना *kose kíáná.*	साप देना.
Curse, *n.*	बखिया *bakhiyá.*	साप.
Custom, *n.*	नेंग *neṇg.*	रीति, व्यवहार.
Cut, *v.*	अस्काना *askáná,* कोईआना *koíáná.*	काटना, घास काटना
Dam (bank), *n.*	मोंगा *moṇgá.*	मोहरी.
—(in a river), *n.*	कट्टा *kaṭṭá.*	पाड़.
Dam up, *v.*	कट्टा कहताना *kaṭṭá kahtáná.*	पाड़ बांधना.
Damp, *adj.*	वट्ताल *waṭṭál.*	गीला, भीगा.
Dance, *v.*	येन्दाना *yendáná,* सेहताना *sehtáná.*	नाचना.
Darkness, *n.*	सीकाटी *síkáṭí,* अन्धेरा *andherá.*	अन्धेरा.
Date tree, *n.*	छतलासींदी *chhatlá-[síṇdí.*	छुहारा.
Daughter, *n.*	मीआर *miár.*	बेटी.
— -in-law, *n.*	कोड़िआड़ *koṛiáṛ.*	बहू.
Dawn, *n.*	कुरकूसे *kurkúse.*	भोर.
Day, *n.*	दिन *din,* पिआल *piál.*	दिन.
— after to-morrow, *n.*	मन्ने *manne.*	परसों.
— third, *past* or *future.*	हरने *harne.*	नरसों.

English.	Gondi.	Hindi.
Day, fourth, *p.* or *future.*	पिरने *pirne.*	चौथा दिन.
— fifth, *past* or *future.*	सरने *sarne.*	पांचवा दिन.
Dead, *adj.*	साताल *sátál.*	मरा हुआ.
Decay, *v.*	कड़ीसाना *kaṛísáná.*	सड़ना.
Deceive, *v.*	चक्का कीआना *chakká kíáná.*	धोखा देना.
Deception, *n.*	मीसा *mísá.*	मिस, बहाना.
Deer, *n.*	माओक *máok.*	हिरण, मृग.
Deity (God), *n.*	भगवान *bhagwán.*	ईशवर, भगवान.
—— (idol), *n.*	पेन *pen.*	देव.
Delay, *n.*	झेर *jher,* अवार *awár.*	देर, बेर.
Demon, *n.*	दैथुर *dáithur.*	भूत.
Demonstrate, *v.*	हुरसहताना *hursah-táná.*	दिखाना.
Den, *n.*	ढोडुर *ḍhoḍur,* मांड़ा *máṇṛá.*	मांड़.
Dense, *adj.*	संघरो *saṅghro.*	घना.
Deprive, *v.*	ऊंचहताना *úṇchah-táná.*	छीनना.
Derision, *n.*	कीरी *kírí.*	टट्टा.
Descend, *v.*	रैयाना *ráiyáná,* रग्गाना *raggáná.*	उतरना.
—— (to cause to), *v.*	रेहटाना *rehṭáná.*	उतारना.

English.	Gondi.	Hindi.
Despatch, *v.*	आवसहताना *áwsahtáná.*	पहुंचाना.
Dew, *n.*	मच *mach.*	ओस.
Dewlap, *n.*	गर्दान *gardán.*	गलाकम्बल.
Ḍhák tree (*Butea frondosa*), *n.*	मुर *mur.*	ढाक, छेऊला.
Dháwá tree (*Gristea tomentosa*), *n.*	अर्मा *armá.*	धावा.
Die, *v.*	सायाना *sáyáná.*	मरना.
Diet, *n.*	टोला *ṭolá.*	भोजन.
Dig, *v.*	कोचिहताना *kochihtáná,* कताना *kátáná.*	खोदना.
Dip, *v.*	मुरहची सीआना *murahchí síáná,* मुरीसाना *murísáná.*	डुबाना.
Direction, *n.*	पट्टी *paṭṭí.*	तरफ़.
Disciple, *n.*	बरूआ *baruá.*	पंडा का चेला.
Dismiss, *v.*	हन्दा सीआना *handá síáná,* पोहची सीआना *pohchí síáná.*	जाने देना.
Distribute, *v.*	तूसी सीआना *túsí* [*síáná.*	बांट देना.

English.	Gondi.	Hindi.
Disturb, *v.*	खिसे कीआना *khise kíáná.*	खिझाना, छेड़ना.
Do, *v.*	कीआना *kíáná.*	करना.
Doe, *n.*	डाड़ी *ḍáṛí.*	हिरणी.
Dog, *n.*	नै *nái,* सिट्टी *siṭṭí.*	कुत्ता, कुत्ती.
Done, to be, managed, *v.*	तूनाना *túnáná.*	बनना.
Double, *adj.*	नड़पा *naṛpá.*	दोहरा.
Dove, *n.*	पुर्राज *purráj.*	पंड़की.
Down (of birds), *n.*	बूईया *búíyá,* माड़े *máṛe.*	रोम.
Doze, *v.*	कुर्कीना *kurkíná.*	ऊंघना.
Drag, *v.*	वीस्काना *wískáná,* अर्रीताना *arrítáná.*	खेंचना, ले आना.
Draw water, *v.*	उमाना *umáná.*	पानी निकालना.
Dress(of men)*v.*	पोन्दाना *pondáná.*	पहिनना (पुरुषों के विषय में).
—(of women)*v.*	ऊहताना *úhtáná.*	पहिनना (स्त्रीयोंके विषय में.)
Drink, *v.*	उन्दाना *undáná.*	पीना.
—(to make to)*v.*	ऊहताना *úhtáná.*	पिलाना.
Drive in (as a stake), *v.*	उरसहताना *ursahtáná.*	गाड़ना.
Driven in (to be,) *v.*	उरसाना *ursáná.*	गड़ना.
Dry, *adj.*	वत्ताल *wattál.*	सूखा.

English.	Gondi.	Hindi.
Dry, *v. i.*	वत्ताना *wattáná.*	सूखना.
— *v. t.*	वहचहताना *wah-chahtáná.*	सूखाना.
Dung (cow), *n.*	सड़ापी *saṛápí.*	गोबर.
Dust, *n.*	धुर्रो *dhurro.*	धूळ.
Each, *pron.*	उन्दीउन्दी *undí undí,* वक्को वक्को *wakko wakko.*	एक एक.
Eagle, *n.*	गिधाल *gidhál.*	गिध.
Ear, *n.*	कवी *kawí.*	कान.
— (lobe of the), *n.*	लाटीकवी *láṭíkawí.*	कान का झुलता हुआ मांस.
Earn, *v.*	कमे कीआना *kame kíáná.*	कमाना.
Ear-ring, *n.*	तारी *tárí.*	झुमका, कान के [गहने.
Earth, *n.*	तोड़ी *toṛí.*	मिट्टी.
Ease oneself, *v.*	पेलाना *peláná.*	हगना.
Eat, *v.*	तिन्दाना *tindáná.*	खाना.
Edge, *n.*	आछी *áchhí.*	आंचल, किनारा.
Egg, *n.*	मेंड *meṇḍ,* मेस्क *mesk.*	अंडा, अंडे.
Elbow, *n.*	कुन्द गोहनी *kund gohní,* कुन्दागोह *kundágoh.*	कुहनी.
Elephant, *n.*	ऐनी *áiní.* [*gane.*	हाथी.
Elsewhere, *adv.*	उड़े बग्गने *uṛe bag-*	और कहीं.

English.	Gondi.	Hindi.
Empty, *adj.*	सूनो *súno*, रित्तो *ritto.*	सूना.
—— *v.*	रित्तो कीआना *ritto kíáná.* [*táná.*	सूना करना.
Enclose, *v.*	वल्लहताना *wallah-*	रूंधना.
End, *n.*	छोर *chhor.* [*táná.*	अन्त.
Enlarge, *v.*	वीरसहताना *wírsah-*	बड़ा करना, बढ़ाना.
Enter, *v.*	सोड़िताना *soṛitáná.*	पैठना.
Envy, *v.*	कड़वीताना *kaṛwí-táná.* [*ná.*	डाह करना.
Erect, *v.*	निलहताना *nilahtá-*	खड़ा करना.
Err, *v.*	मरगीना *margíná.*	भूलना.
Escape, *v.*	पिस्साना *pissáná.*	बचना.
Evade, *v.*	पसीसी डायाना *pasísí*	निकलके भागना.
Even, *adv.*	गदा *gadá.* [*ḍáyáná.*	वैसाही, भी.
Evening, *n.*	नुल्पे *nulpe.*	सांझ.
Ever, *adv.* [*adv.*	बप्पोरे *bappore.*	कभी.
Everywhere,	बग्गने *baggane.*	हर कहीं
Except, *prep.*	पोहची *pohchí.*	छोड़के.
Excrement, *n.*	पींग *píṇg.* [*kíáná.*	गुह, गू.
Expand, *v.*	बगड़े कीआना *bagṛe*	फैलाना.
Expel, *v.*	खेदे कीआना *khede kíáná.*	खदेड़ना.
Extinguish, *v.*	पिहताना *pihtáná.*	बुझाना.
— ed (to be), *v.*	पिराना *piráná.*	बुझना.
Eye, *n.* [the), *n.*	कन *kan.*	आंख.
— (pupil of	कावा *káwá.*	आंख की पुतली.

English.	Gondi.	Hindi.
Eye (dirt in the),	चिपड़ींग *chipṛíṇg.*	आंख में मैल.
Eyebrow, *n.* [*n.*	वट्टे *waṭṭe,* कुन्कुन्दा *kunkundá.*	भौं, भृकुटि.
Eyelash, *n.*	मिन्दी *mindí.*	बरोनी.
Eyelid, *n.*	कन तिपली *kan tiplí.*	पलक, पपोटा.
Fall, *v.*	अर्राना *arráná,* मीड़ाना *míṛáná.*	गिरना.
Family, *n.*	कुड़मा *kuṛmá.*	कुरमा, कुटुम्ब.
Famish, *v.* [*n.*	करू सायाना *karú* [*sáyáná.*	भूखों मरना.
Fan, winnowing	सेती *setí.*	सूप.
Far, *adv.*	लख *lakh.*	दूर.
Fat, *adj.*	कुरवींज *kurwíṇj.*	मोटा (पशुओं के [विषय में).
Father, *n.* [*n.*	दादाल *dádál.*	पिता.
Father-in-law,	मुर्या *muryá.*	ससुर.
Fear, *n.*	वर्री *warrí.*	डर.
Feather, *n.*	मारे *máre.*	पर, पंख.
Feed, *v.*	तिहताना *tihtáná.*	खिलाना.
Female, *n.*	आर *ár,* माई *máí.*	स्त्री.
Fence, *n.*	वेड़ा *weṛá,* कीरी *kírí.*	टट्टी.
Fever, *n.*	अर्की *arkí.*	ज्वर, तप.
Few, *adj.*	अमू *amú,* हमू *hamú.*	थोड़े.
Field, *n.*	नेली *nelí,* नेल *nel.*	खेत.
Fig, *n.*	तोया *toyá.*	गूलर.
Fill, *v.*	निहताना *nihtáná.*	भर देना.
Fill in earth, *v.*	मुहताना *muhtáná.*	मारी भरना.

English.	Gondi.	Hindi.
Filled (to be), *v.*	निन्नताना *ninnatáná.*	भरना.
Find, *v.* [*adj.*	पुट्टाना *puṭṭáná.*	मिलना.
Fine (of texture)	झीनोर *jhínor.*	महीन.
Finish, *v.*	कीसी येताना *kísí yetáná,* माहताना *máhtáná.*	पूरा करना, सिद्ध करना.
Fire, *n.*	किस *kis.*	आग.
Firefly, *n.*	मिन्को *minko.*	जुगनू.
First, *adj.*	पहिलो *pahilo.*	पहिला.
Fish, *n.*	मीन *mín.*	मछली.
— frame for catching, *n.*	घुस्सुर *ghussur.*	मछली पकड़ने का ठाठ.
Five (number)	सैयूंग *sáiyúṇg.*	पांच.
Flax, *n.*	बैयाल *báiyál.*	सन.
Flea, *n.*	पित्ता *pittá.*	पिस्सू.
Flee, *v.*	डैसी हन्दाना *ḍáisí handáná,* जड़ीताना *jaṛítáná.*	भाग जाना.
Fling, *v.*	नच्छाना *nachchháná*	फेंकना.
Float away, *v.*	पोंगाना *poṇgáná.*	बहना.
Flood, *n.*	ऊसा *úsá.*	बाढ़.
Flour, *n.*	पिन्दी *pindí.*	आटा.
Flower, *n.*	पुंगार *puṇgár.*	फूल.
—— *v.*	पूईना *púíná,* पोड़ीना [*poṛíná*	फूलना.
Fly, *n.*	वीसी *wísí.*	मक्खी.
— *v.*	पोरीताना *porítáná.*	उड़ना.

English.	Gondi.	Hindi.
Foot, *n.*	काल *kál.*	पांव.
Forest, *n.*	डोंगुर *ḍoṇgur.*	जंगल.
Forget, *v.*	मरूंगसीआना *ma-ruṇgsíáná.*	भूल जाना.
Fork (hay), *n.*	कुरेली *kurelí.*	कांटा घास उड़ाने को.
Four (number), *n.*	नालूंग *nálúṇg.*	चार.
Fowl, *n.*	खुर्र *khurr.*	मुर्गी.
—(half-grown)	पोई *poí,* पोईंज *poíṇj.*	आधी मुर्गी.
Fox, *n.*	कुसत्ती *kusattí.*	लोमड़ी.
Frighten, *v.*	वर्रहताना *warrah-táná.*	डराना.
Frog, *n.*	पन्ने *panne.*	मेंडक.
From, *prep.*	-ताल *-tál,* -टाल *-ṭál,* -हड़ा *-haṛá.*	से.
Frost (hoar), *n.*	तुस्सार *tussár.*	पाला.
Froth, *n.*	लार *lár.*	फेन.
Fuel, *n.*	छूई *chhúí.*	ईंधन, पतली लकड़ी.
Full, *adj.*	मेण्ड़ *meṇṛ.*	भर.
Furrow, *n.*	कूढ़ *kúṛh.*	कूंढ.
Gate, *n.*	फड़का *phaṛká.*	फाटक.
Gaze, *v.*	नादीना *nádíná.*	देख रहना.
Ghee, *n.*	पालनी *pální.*	घी.
Girl, *n.*	पेड़गी *peṛgí.*	लड़की.
Give, *v.*	सीआना *síáná.*	देना.
Glean, *v.*	पहकाना *pahkáná.*	बिनना.
Gleanings, *n.*	सीला *sílá.*	जो बिना जाता है.

English.	Gondi.	Hindi.
Glutton, *n.*	डर्गाल *ḍargál.*	पेटू.
Gnat, *n.*	नुल्ले *nulle.*	मच्छड़.
Go, *v.*	हन्दाना *handáná.*	जाना.
— over, *v.*	अहकाना *ahkáná.*	पार उतरना.
Goat, *n.*	येटी *yeṭí.*	बकड़ी.
— (young), *n.*	बरई *baraí.*	बकड़ी का बच्चा.
Gold, *n.*	सोनो *sono.*	सोना.
Gond, *n.*	कोइतोर *koitor.*	गोंड़.
Gondi, *n.*	कोइयां *koiyáṇ.*	गोंड़ी भाषा.
Gondin, *n.*	कोइतार *koitár.*	गोंड़िन.
Good, *adj.*	बेश *besh,* चोखो *cho-kho.*	अच्छा.
Gore, *v.*	कोहकाना *kohkáná.*	कोंचना.
Gourd, *n.*	परास *parás.*	लौकी.
Grain-pit, *n.*	खौंड़ी *khouṇṛí,* कोठी *koṭhí.*	खौं.
Gram, *n.*	हनऐक *hanaáik.*	चना.
Grandfather, *n.*	आजाल *ájál.*	दादा.
—— great, *n.*	अक्को *akko.*	दादा का पिता.
Grass, *n.*	जाड़ी *jáṛí.*	घास.
Grasshopper, *n.*	फाफे *pháphe.*	टिड्डा.
Grave, *n.*	मर्घट *marghaṭ.*	समाधि.
Graze, *v. t.*	मेहताना *mehtáná.*	चराना.
Grind, *v.*	नोर्राना *norráná.*	पीसना.
Groan, *v.*	कहली कीआना *kahlí kíáná.*	कहरना.

English.	Gondi.	Hindi.
Grow (of plants), *v.*	पिरीना *piríná*, बोरसाना *borsáná.*	उगना.
Guest, *n.*	वर्त्ताल *warttál.*	पाहुन.
Hail, *n.*	ओरा *orá.*	ओला.
Hair, *n.*	चुट्टिंग *chuṭṭiṇg.*	बाल.
Hand, *n.*	कै *kái.*	हाथ.
Hang, *v. i.*	उरमे मायाना *urme máyáná.*	लटकना.
—— *v. t.*	कोंचे कीआना *koṇche kíáná.*	लटकाना.
Hare, *n.*	मोलोल *molol.*	खर्गोश.
Harvest, *n.*	कोईआना *koíáná.*	लवने का काल.
Hatching (hen), [*n.*	काड़ा *káṛá.*	सेवती हुई मुर्गी.
He, *pron.*	ओर *or.*	वह.
Head, *n.*	तला *talá.*	सिर.
Heap, *n.*	रास *rás*, रासी *rásí.*	ढेर.
—— *v.*	सूर कीआना *súr kíáná.*	ढेर करना.
Hear, *v.*	केंजाना *keṇjáná.*	सुनना.
Heat (sun's), *n.*	अदी *adí.*	घाम, धूप.
Heat, *v.*	कासाना *kásáná*, कासहताना *kásahtáná.*	गरम करना, तपाना.
Heaven, *n.*	बैकुण्ट *báikuṇṭ*, जामू दीप *jámú díp.*	परलोक, बैकुण्ट.

English.	Gondi.	Hindi.
Heavy, *adj.*	पोहटा *pohṭá.*	भारी.
Heel, *n.*	डांका *ḍáṇká.*	एड़ी.
Heifer, *n.*	पड्डा *paḍḍá.*	बछिया.
Hell, *n.*	नरक *narak.*	पाताल.
Hence, *adv.*	इग्गाटाल *iggáṭál,* इग्गाहड़ा *iggáhaṛá.*	यहां से.
Herdsman, *n.*	कोपाल *kopál.*	अहीर.
Here, *adv.*	इग्गा *iggá.*	यहां.
Hide, *v.i.*	मक्काना *makkáná.*	छिप जाना.
— *v. t.*	मकसहताना *maksahtáná.*	छिपाना.
High, *adj.*	लम्बो *lambo,* बड्डी *baddí.*	ऊंचा.
Hill, *n.*	कुड़ *kuṛu.*	टीला.
Him, *pron.*	ओॅन *on.*	उसको.
Hindi, *n.*	कोष *kosh.*	हिन्दी भाषा.
Hindu man, *n.*	कोषुर *koshur.*	हिन्दू पुरुष.
— woman, *n.*	कोषतार *koshtár.*	हिन्दू स्त्री.
Hireling, *n.*	कबाड़ेक *kabáṛek.*	ठिकहा.
Hither, *adv.*	हिक्के *hikke.*	इधर.
Hole, *n.*	छड़का *chhaṛká,* दसना *dasná.*	छेद.
Hone, *n.*	मसान *masán.*	सान.
Honey, *n.*	कानल *kánal.*	मधु.
Horn, *n.*	कोर *kor.*	सिंग.
Horse, *n.*	कोड़ा *koṛá.*	घोड़ा.
Hot, *adj.*	कास्ताल *kástál.*	गरम, तप्त.

English.	Gondi.	Hindi.
House, *n.*	रोन *ron.*	घर.
How? *adv.*	बहबा *bahbá.*	कैसा.
How many? *adv.*	बचाले *bachále.*	कितने.
Hunger, *n.*	करू *karú.*	भूख.
Husband, *n.*	मोइदो *moido.*	पति.
—'s brother, *n.*	सीरन्दू *sírandú.*	पति का भाई.
Hut, *n.*	झाला *jhálá.*	झोपड़ी.
I, *pron.*	नन्ना *nanná.*	मैं.
Illness, *n.*	बिजारी *bijárí.*	बीमारी.
In, *prep.*	-टे *-ṭe,* -ते *-te.*	में.
Insect, *n.*	पुड़ी *puṛí.*	कीड़ा.
Insert, *v.*	कोंचेकी सीआना *koṇcheki siáná.*	डाल देना.
Inside, *prep.*	रोपा *ropá.*	भीतर.
Instruct, *v.*	करहताना *karahtá-ná.*	सिखाना.
Intrude, *v.*	नंगाना *neṇgáná.*	घुस जाना.
Iron, *n.*	कच्ची *kachchí.*	लोहा.
It, *pron.*	अद *ad.*	यह, वह.
Itch, *n.*	खस *khas.*	खुजली, खाज.
Jackal, *n.*	कोल्हयाल *kolhayál.*	सियाल, लड़ैया.
Jar (earthen), *n.*	कुरवी *kurwí.*	घड़ा.
Jester, *n.*	करबाल *karbál.*	ठठोल.
Jugnu, *n.*	कोइतार *koitár.*	जुगनू.

English.	Gondi.	Hindi.
Junhárí, *n.*	ज्वार्क *jwárk.*	जुनहारी.
Kacharia (*Hedychium spicatum*), *n.*	बोदेला *bodelá.*	कचरी.
Khalí, *n.*	पाकी *pákí*, ढेप *ḍhep.*	खली.
Khamer tree (*Gmelina arborea*).	खुर्सी *khursí.*	खमेर, खुमहेर.
Khichaṛi, (*Zizyphus jujuba*), [*n.*	लपसा *lapsá.*	खिचड़ी.
Kill, *v.*	जोहकाना *johkáná*, जीआना *jíáná.*	मारडालना, मारना.
Kiss, *v.*	नोंडाना *noṇḍáná.*	चूमना.
Knead, *v.*	पिस्काना *piskáná.*	सानना.
Knee, *n.*	मुरटोला *murṭolá.*	घुट[illegible].
Kneecap, *n.*	टवड़ी *ṭawaṛí.*	घुटने की चक्की.
Know, *v.*	पुन्दाना *pundáná.*	जानना.
Kodo-grain (*Paspalum Kora*), *n.*	कुद्दां *kuddáṇ.*	कोदों.
Kush-grass, *n.*	घानाड़ी *ghánáṛí.*	कूश घास.
Kutki-grain (*Panicum miliare*), *n.*	कोहला *kohalá.*	कुटकी.

English.	Gondi.	Hindi.
Laugh, *v.*	कंवाना *kaṇwáná.*	हसना.
Lazy, *adj.*	कुढ़ियाल *kuṛhiyál.*	आलसी.
Lead, *v.*	मुन्ने ताकीना *munne tákíná.*	आगे चलना.
Leaf, *n.*	आकी *ákí.*	पत्ता.
Leak, *v.*	वड़ाना *waṛáná.*	चूना.
Leap, *v.*	डहकाना *ḍahkáná.*	कूदना.
Learn, *v.*	कर्रिताना *karritáná.*	सीखना.
Leather, *n.*	तोल *tol.*	चमड़ा.
Leg, *n.*	पोटरी *poṭarí.*	टांग, गोड़.
Lentil, *n.*	दारी *dárí.*	दाल.
Leopard, *n.*	चीताल *chítál.*	चीता.
Liar, *n.*	लबड़ाल *labṛál.*	लबाड़, झूठा.
Lick, *v.*	नाकीना *nákíná.*	चाटना.
Lid, *n.*	मुच्छे *muchchhe.*	ढकना.
Lie down (of animals), *v.*	पट्टीना *paṭṭíná.*	लेटना (पशुओं के विषय में).
Light, *n.*	वेड़ची *weṛchí.*	ज्योति.
Light, *adj.*	अखड़ो *akhaṛo.*	हलका.
Lighten (flash), *v.*	मिरसालना *mirsálná.*	चमकना.
Lightning, *n.*	गाज *gáj.*	बिजली.
Like, *prep.*	घाईं *ghaiṇ.*	समान, नाई.
Lip, *n.*	सिलवी *silwí.*	ओंठ.
Little, *adj.*	छुडोर *chhuḍor.*	छोटा.
——— *a.*	अमुहच *amuhach.*	थोड़ा सा.
Live, *v.*	पिस्साना *pissáná.*	जीना.
Liver, *n.*	तड़ाकी *taṛákí.*	कलेजा.

English.	Gondi.	Hindi.
Lizard, *n.*	उर्रुम *urrum.*	छिपकली.
——— (large), *n.*	डोक्के *ḍokke.*	गिरगिट.
Log (of wood), *n.*	डूंड़ा *ḍúṇṛá.* [*ni.*	लक्कड़.
Loins, *n.*	नन *nan,* नन्नी *nan-*	कमर, कटि.
Loose (cattle), *v.*	तासाना *tásáná.*	छूटा देना.
Loosed (to be), *v.*	रेंगीना *reṇginá.*	छूटना.
Lose (the way) *v.*	बहके मायाना *bahke máyáná.*	भटक जाना, भूलना.
Lota (a brass vessel), *n.*	चरू *charú.*	लोटा.
Louse, *n.*	बोत्ता *bottá.* [*paṛkí.*	जूं.
———'s eggs, *n.*	सीर्के *sírk,* पड़की	लीख.
Lungs, *n.*	पिपसा *pipsá,* पिस्ता *pistá.*	फेफड़े.
Mad, *adj.*	बैहाल *báihál.*	बावला.
Mahulain creeper (*Bauhinia Vahlii*), *n.*	पाउर *páur.*	महुलाइन.
Mahua tree (*Bassia latifolia*), *n.*	इड़ू *iṛú.*	महुआ.
Maina bird (*Gracula religiosa*) *n.*	सालो *sálo.*	मैना.
Maize, *n.*	जन्ना *janná.*	भुट्टा.
Man, *n.*	मान्वाल *mánwál,* माड़साल *máṛsál.*	मनुष्य.

English.	Gondi.	Hindi.
Mangoe tree (*Mangifera Indica*), *n.*	मरका *marká.*	आम.
Mankind, *n.*	माड़सालोर *máṛsálor.*	मनुष्यजाति.
Manure, *n.*	खर्सी *kharsí.*	खाद.
Many *adj.*	वल्ले *walle.*	बहुत.
As many as	बच्चो *bachcho.*	जितने.
Market, *n.*	हाटुम *háṭum.*	बाज़ार, हाट.
Marriage, *n.* [*n.*	मड़मीं *maṛmíṇ.*	बिवाह.
Masúr (*cicerlens*)	मसूर्क *masúrk.*	मसूर की दाल.
Mat, *n.*	कत्ती *kattí.*	चटाई.
Meal, early morning.	बसिया *basiyá.*	तड़के का भोजन.
— ten o'clock.	जावा *jáwá.*	दस बजे का भोजन.
— three o'clock.	मड़ैया *maṛáiyá.*	तीन बजे का भोजन.
— evening.	बियारी *biyárí.*	सांझ का भोजन.
Mean, *adj.*	ऊतार *útár.*	नीच.
Meat, *n.*	संवी *saṇwí.*	मांस.
Medicine, *n.*	मत *mat.* [*táná.*	दवा, औषध.
Meet, *v.*	पुरसहताना *pursah-*	मिल जाना.
Melt, *v.*	घुरे मायाना *ghure máyáná*, कड़ीताना *kaṛítáná.*	गल जाना.
Mend, *v.*	साजी कीआना *sáji kíáná.*	संवारना, सुधारना.
Mid-day, *n.*	धूपर *dhúpar.*	दो पहर.

English.	Gondi.	Hindi.
Milk, *n.*	पाल *pál.*	दूध.
—— *v.*	पीराना *piráná.*	दुहना.
Mill (hand), *n.*	जत्ता *jattá.*	चक्की.
Mist, *n.*	कूहरा *kúhará.*	कुहासा.
Mix, *v.*	खोई कीआना *khoí kiáná.*	मिलाना.
Moan, *n.*	धांई *dháṇí.*	बिलाप, हाहाकार.
Moon, *n.*	चन्दमाल *chandarmál,* नलेंज *naleṇj*	चन्द्रमा, चान्द.
More, *adv.*	उड़े *uṛe.*	और, अधिक.
Morning, *n.*	बुनसारी *bunsárí,* सकाड़ी *sakáṛí.*	बिहान, प्रातहकाल.
Morrow, *n.*	नर्कईं *narkaiṇ.*	कल.
Mortar, *n.*	सहकी *sahkí.*	उखली.
Moss, *n.*	बुच्छी *buchchhí.*	काई.
Mother, *n.*	दाई *dái,* अवहरी *awharí.*	माता, मा.
—— -in-law, *n.*	पोयार *poyár.*	सास.
Mountain, *n.*	मट्टा *maṭṭá.*	पहाड़.
Mouse, *n.*	अल्ली *allí.*	चूहा.
Mouth, *n.*	टुडी *ṭuḍí.*	मुंह.
Much, *adj., adv.*	नक्का *nakká.*	बहुत, बहुतसा.
As much as	बच्चोर *bachchor.*	जितना.
Mud, *n.*	चिकला *chiklá.*	कीचड़.
Mundi grain (*Sphæranthus Indicus*), *n.*	कैमा *káimá.*	मुरडी.

English.	Gondi.	Hindi.
Musk-rat, *n.*	छूचो *chhúcho.*	छचून्दर.
Must, *v.*	चाही *cháhí.*	चाहिये.
Mustard.	सरसवा *sarsawá.*	सरसों.
My, *pron.*	नावोर *náwor,* नावा *náwá.*	मेरा, मेरी.
Nail (finger), *n.*	तिरींज *tiriṇj.*	नख.
Naked (to be), *v.*	कुराके मायाना *kurá-ke máyáná.*	नंगा होना.
Name, *n.*	पड़ोल *paṛol.*	नाम.
—— *v.*	पड़ोल वीसाना *paṛol wisáná.*	नाम लगाना.
Navel, *n.*	गुदि *gudi.* [*muṭis.*	नाभी.
Near, *prep., adv.*	करूम *karrum,* मुटिस	निकट, पास.
Neck, *n.*	घोंगा *ghoṇgá,* वरेर *warer.*	गर्दन, गला.
— (nape of), *n.*	गिछरी *gichharí.*	गुद्दी.
Necklace (men's), *n.*	दुम्मे *dumme.*	माला पुरुषोंका.
— (women's), *n.*	पोती *potí.*	माला स्त्रीयोंका.
Nephew, *n.*	सन्नीमर्री *sannímarrí.*	भतीजा, भांझा.
Nerve, *n.*	चीरा *chírá.*	नाड़ी, सिरा.
Nest, *n.*	गोदा *godá.* [*hille.*	घोंसला.
Never, *adj.*	बप्पुरे हिल्ले *bappure*	कभी नहीं.
New, *adj.*	नमतल *namtal,* पूनल *púnal.*	नया.
Night, *n.*	नर्का *narká.*	रात.

English.	Gondi.	Hindi.
No, *adv.*	हिल्ले *hille,* मिन्ने *minne.*	नहीं, मत.
Nod, *v.*	नवे कीआना *nawe kíáná.*	सिर झुकाना, नवाना.
Noise, *n.*	लेंग *leṇg.*	शब्द.
None, *adj.*	बद्दे हिल्ले *badde hille.*	कोई नहीं.
Nose, *n.*	मस्सोर *massor.*	नाक.
— (bridge of) *n.*	नखदण्डी *nakhdanḍí*	
Now, *adv.*	इंगा *iṇgá,* इन्देके *indeke,* इसारी *isárí.*	अब, अभी.
Nowhere, *adv.*	बग्गने हिल्ले *baggane hille.*	कहीं नहीं.
Number, *v.*	काहताना *káhtáná.*	गिनना.
Offspring, *n.*	छौवा पूटां *chhouwá púṭáṇ.*	लड़केवाले.
Oil, *n.*	नी *ní.*	तेल.
— vessel, *n.*	डुड़वा *ḍuṛawá.*	बोर.
Old, *adj.*	जुन्नाल *junnál.*	पुराना.
On, *prep.*	पर्रो *parro.*	पर.
One, (number)	उन्दी *undí.*	एक.
Onion, *n.*	उल्ली *ullí,* गोंडली *goṇḍlí.*	पियाज़.
Open, *adj.*	उगड़े मातल *ugaṛe mátal.*	खुला हुआ.
Or, *conj.*	धों *dhoṇ.*	या, वा.
Order, *v.*	कच्ची सीआना *kachchí síáná.*	आज्ञा देना.
Our, *pron.*	मावोर *máwor,* मावा *máwá.*	हमारा, हमारी.
Oven, *n.*	सदोली *sadolí.*	चूल्हा.

English.	Gondi.	Hindi.
Owl, *n.*	फूसरा *phúsará.*	उल्लू.
Pagri, *n.*	फेटा *pheṭá.*	पगड़ी.
Pair, *n.* [*n.*	रण्डे *randé*, रण्टे *ranṭe.*	जोड़े, दोनों.
Pankha (caste),	गांड़ाल *gáṇṛál.*	पंखा जाति.
Parched grain, *n*	फूटांग *phuṭáṇg.*	भूंजा हुआ अनाज.
Pardhan (caste),	पानाल *pánál.*	परधान.
Parrot, *n.* [*n.*	सिड़ी *siṛí*, माटे *máṭe.*	सूआ, तोता.
Part, *n.*	तूस *tús.*	भाग, टुकड़ा.
Partridge, *n.*	ककरांझ *kakráṇj.*	तीतर.
Pass out, *v.*	पपीताना *papítáná.*	निकल जाना.
Patch, *n.*	थिगड़ा *thigṛá.*	कपड़े का टुकड़ा.
Path, *n.*	सरी *sarí.*	रास्ता, मार्ग.
Pea, *n.*	बुटरा *buṭará.*	मटर.
Peacock, *n.*	मल *mal.*	मोर.
Penjh (cooked food), *n.*	जावा *jáwá.*	पेंझ.
Perhaps, *adv.*	बसेकने *basekne.*	कदाचित.
Perspiration, *n.*	ईपुर *ípur.*	पसीना.
Pestle, *n.*	उस्काल *uskál.*	मूसल.
Pig, *n.*	पद्दी *paddí.*	सूअर.
— (devoted to Narayan Deo), *n.*	लाड़ो *láṛo.*	जो नरायन को चढ़ाया जाएगा.

English.	Gondi.	Hindi.
Pig (devoted to the sun), *n.*	सुरजाल *surjál.*	जो सूरज को चढ़ाया जाएगा.
Pigeon, *n.*	पारेवा *párewá*, हरला *harlá.*	कबूतर, हारिल.
Pillar, *n.*	सरा *sará.*	खंभा.
Pipal tree (*Ficus religiosa*), *n.*	आली *álí.*	पीपल.
Pipe (for smoking), *n.*	चिलम *chilam.*	चिलम.
Pit, *n.*	कुदरा *kudrá.*	कूंड, गढ़ा.
Pitcher, *n.*	सोरा *sorá.*	घड़ा.
—— red (for water), *n.*	मल्ला *mallá.*	लाल घड़ा.
—— black (for cooking), *n.*	कुड़वी *kuṛwí.*	काला घड़ा.
Place, *v.*	इर्राना *irráná.*	रखना.
Plate, *n.*	धनिया *dhaniyá.*	थाली.
—— of leaves, *n.*	कूनी *kúní.*	पत्तों का पात्र.
—— of leaves, (small), *n.*	डुप्पा *ḍuppá.*	पत्तों का छोटा पात्र.
Play, *v.*	कर्साना *karsáná.*	खेलना.
Plough, *v.*	उड़ाना *uṛáná.*	जोतना.
—— *n.*	नांगेल *náṅgel.*	हल.
Pod, *n.*	सेंगा *seṇgá.*	छीमी.
Poison, *n.*	माहुर *máhur.*	विष, माहुर.
Pork, *n.*	पद्दी ता संवी *paddí tá saṇwí.*	सूअर का मांस.

English.	Gondi.	Hindi.
Pound, *v.*	उस्साना *ussáná.*	कूटना, पीसना.
Pour, *v.*	कोहरे कीआना *kohare kíáná.* [सीआना *síáná.*]	बहाना.
—— out, *v.*	तोरसी सीआना *torsí síáná.*	उंडेलना.
Powerful, *adj.*	साबुर *sábur.*	प्रबल, बली.
Preach, *v.*	वहताना *wahtáná,* केंचहताना *keṇchahtáná.*	बताना, सुनाना.
Press, *v.*	अदमाना *admáná.*	दबाना.
Pull, *v.*	वीस्काना *wískáná.*	खैंचना.
Put, *v.*	दोस्साना *dossáná.*	धरना.
—— out, *v.*	ठंड़ाना *ṭhaṇṛáná.*	निकालना.
Putrid, *adj.*	सौवताल *souwtál.*	सड़ा.
Quail, *n.*	ऊती *útí.*	बटेर.
Quarrel, *v.*	तरेहताना *tarehtáná.*	लड़ना.
Quickly, *adv.*	जपने *japne,* निची निची *nichí nichí.*	जलदी.
Rag, *n.*	पड़या *paṛyá.*	चिपड़ा.
Rain, *n.*	पिर्र *pirr.*	मेंह.
Rainbow, *n.*	गोरा *gorá.*	रामधनुष.
Raw, *adj.*	पाहनाल *páhnál.*	कच्चा.
Razor, *n.*	मजिआ *majiá.*	उस्तुरा, छूरा.
Reach, *v.*	अव्वाना *awwáná.*	पहुंचना.
Reap, *v.*	कुय्याना *kuyyáná.*	लवना, काटना.
Receive, *v.*	येताना *yetáná.*	लेना.

English.	Gondi.	Hindi.
Reed-pen, *n.*	मरिआ *mariá.* [*ná.*	भरू.
Rend, *v.*	सरहतना *sarrahtá-*	फाड़ना.
Rent, *p. part.*	सर्त *sart.* [*ná.*	फाड़ा हुआ.
Rescue, *v.*	पिसेहताना *pisehtá-*	बचाना. [लेना.
Rest, *v.*	रोमीना *rominá.*	सुस्ताना, विश्राम
Return, *v.*	मल्लाना *malláná.*	लौटना.
Reveal, *v.*	हूड़सहताना *húṛsah-*	दिखाना.
Rice (in field), *n.*	वंजी *waṇjí.* [*táná.*	धान.
— (in grain), *n.*	परईक *paraík.*	चावल.
— (broken in grinding), *n.*	नूका *núká.*	कन्की.
— (cooked), *n.*	गाटो *gáṭo.*	भात.
Rick, *n.*	पकी *pakí,* पुंजा *punjá*	गंजी.
Ring, *n.*	मुद्दा *muddá.*	अंगूठी.
Ripe, *adj.*	पंड़तल *paṇṛtal.*	पक्का.
—— (to be), *v.*	पण्डीना *panḍíná.*	पक जाना.
Roast, *v.*	बुर्साना *bursáná.*	भूनना.
Root, *n.*	सीड़ *síṛ.*	जड़.
—— (up), *v.*	तहक सीअताना *tahak síatáná.*	उखाड़ना.
—— (used in the worship of Baṛá Deo), *n.*	नन्द माटी *nand máṭí.*	एक तरह का खान्दा.
Rope (with which cattle are tied), *n.*	दामनी *dámní.*	गिरईया.

English.	Gondi.	Hindi.
Rot, *v. i.*	कड़ीताना *kaṛitáná.*	सड़ना.
— (cause to), *v. t.*	कड़ी सीअताना *kaṛí siatáná.*	सड़ाना.
Rough ground, *n.*	दलहक टिकड़ा *dal-hak ṭikṛá.*	ऊंची नीची भूमि.
Rub, *v.*	सोकाना *sokáná,* मरेहताना *mareh-táná.*	मलना.
Rubbish, *n.*	विआर *wiár.*	कचरा, कूड़ा.
Run, *v.*	विताना *witáná.*	दौड़ना.
— (away), *v.*	डैयाना *ḍáiyáná,* सो-ड़िताना *soṛitáná.*	भागना.
Sacrifice, *v.*	तरहताना *tarahtá-ná,* बधे कीआना *badhe kiáná.*	चढ़ाना, बध करना.
Saddle, *n.*	खोगुर *khogúr.*	खोगोर.
Saj tree (*Terminalia tomentosa*), *n.*	मरू *marú.*	साज.
Sand, *n.*	बारू *bárú.*	बालू.
Sand-fly, *n.*	नुल्ले *nulle.*	भुनगा, मच्छड़.
Say, *v.*	इन्दाना *indáná,* वन्कीना *wankíná,* कत्ताना *kattáná.*	कहना, बोलना.
Schism, *n.*	ओर्ताल *ortál.*	फूटा हुआ.
Scorpion, *n.*	मिच्छो *michchho.*	बिच्छू.

English.	Gondi.	Hindi.
Scratch, *v.* [*v.*	ताड़कीना *táṛkíná.*	खरोटना, नोचना.
— (violently),	कूचीना *kúchíná.*	बल से खरोटना.
Search for, *v.*	मिरहकाना *mirah-káná.*	ढूंढ़ना.
See, *v.*	हूड़ाना *húṛáná,* नाड़ीना *náṛíná.*	देखना.
Seed, *n.*	विज्जा *wijjá.* [*táná.*	बीज.
Seize, *v.*	बैसी तताना *báisí ta-*	पकड़ लेना.
Self (in 2nd & 3rd pers.), *pro.*	तन्ना *tanná,* तन्वा *tanwá.*	अपना.
Sell, *v.*	ममीताना *mamítáná.*	बेचना.
Send, *v.*	रोहताना *rohtáná.*	भेजना.
Set, *v.*	इर्राना *irráná.*	रखना, धरना.
— (of sun), *v.*	मुरीताना *murítáná.*	डूबना.
Seven (number)	येड़ुंग *yeṛúṇg.*	सात.
Sew, *v.*	वल्चाना *walcháná.*	सीना.
Shade, *n.*	धर्मी *dharmí,* अडाम *aḍám.*	छाया, आड़. [दबाना.
Shampoo, *v.*	गोसली कीआना *gos-*	अंगोंको हाथ से
Share, *n.*	तूस *tús.* [*alí kíáná.*	अंश, बांट.
Sharpen, *v.*	मस्सीताना *massítáná*	चोखा करना.
She, *pron.*	अद *ad.*	वह (स्त्रीलिंग).
Sheep, *n.*	गड़ार *gaṛár.*	भेड़ी.
Shelter, *n.*	सोन्दी *sondí.*	आड़.
Shoe, *n.*	सरपो *sarpo.*	जूता, जूती.
— to put on, *v.*	कर्राना *karráná.*	जूती लगाना.

English.	Gondi.	Hindi.
Short (of stature), *adj.*	बुटराल *buṭrál.*	नाटा.
Shoulder, *n.*	सट्टा *saṭṭá.*	कान्धा.
Shut down, *v.*	मुड़िहताना *muṛihtá-ná.*	ढांपना.
Sickle, *n.*	सटाड़ *saṭáṛ.*	हंसुआ.
Side, *n.*	पट्टी *paṭṭí.*	ओर, तरफ.
Silence! *inter.*	कम्मेके *kammeke.*	चुप.
Simple, *adj.*	भोरो *bhoro.*	भोला, भोरा.
Sing, *v.*	वाराना *wáráná.*	गाना.
Sink, *v.*	मुरंगाना *muraṇgáná*	डूबना.
Sister, *n.*	दीदी *dídí.*	बहिन, सखी.
— (younger), *n*	सेलार *selár.*	छोटी बहिन.
— (elder), *n.*	तक्का *takká.*	बड़ी बहिन.
Sit, *v.*	उदीना *udíná.*	बैठना.
— (cause to), *v.*	उच्चहताना *uchchah-táná.*	बैठाना.
Six (number)	सारूंग *sáruṇg.*	छः.
Skin, *n.*	तोल *tol.*	चमड़ा.
Slay, *v.*	जोहकाना *johkáná.*	मार डालना.
Sleep, *n.*	कुर्की *kurkí.*	नीन्द.
— *v.*	सुंजीना *suṇjíná,* नर्मीना *narmíná.*	सोना.
— heavily, *v.*	कुर्कीना *kurkíná.*	ऊंघना.
Slip, *v.*	घसरी मायाना *ghasrí máyáná.*	खिसकना.
Small, *adj.*	छुडोर *chhuḍor.*	छोटा.
Smell, *v. i.*	दैंगाना *dáiṇgáná.*	बास देना.

English.	Gondi.	Hindi.
Smell, *v. t.*	मस्काना *maskáná.*	सूंघना.
Smoke, *n.*	कुस्सो *kusso.*	धूआं.
Snake, *n.*	तरास *tarás.*	सांप.
Snatch, *v.*	ऊमचाना *úmcháná.*	पकड़ना.
Sneeze, *n.*	सगुन *sagun.*	छींक.
Snore, *v.*	मुरीताना *murítáná.*	घुर्राना.
So, *adv.*	ईहुन *íhun,* आहुन *áhun.*	यूं त्यों.
— much.	अच्चोर *achchor,* इच्चोर *ichchor.*	उतना, इतना.
Soak, *v.*	नाहताना *náhtáná.*	भिगाना.
Soft, *adj.*	कोपे *kope.*	कोमल, चिकना.
Sole (of the foot)	तरूपांव *tarúpáṇw.*	तलुआ.
Somebody, *pron.*	बोरे *bore.*	कोई.
Son, *n.*	मर्री *marrí.*	बेटा.
— -in-law, *n.*	सन्ने *sanne.*	भर्त्ता, दामाद.
—— on probation.	लम्जना *lamjaná.*	जो दामाद होने की आशामें टहल करता है.
—'s wife, *n.*	कोरियार *koriyár.*	बहू.
Song, *n.*	पाटा *páṭá.*	गीत.
Sour, *adj.*	कईताल *kaítál.*	कड़ुआ, खट्टा.
Sow, *v.*	वीताना *witáná.*	बोना.
Space (to have) *v.*	पोड्डाना *poḍḍáná.*	समाना.
Spark, *n.*	बिराम *birám.*	चिंगारी.
Speak, *v.*	वन्कीना *wankíná.*	बोलना.
Spew, *v.*	कोक्कीना *kokkíná* उचरे कीआना *uchre kíáná*	छांट करना.

English.	Gondi.	Hindi.
Spill, *v.*	पोंगीताना *poṇgítáná*	बहाना.
Spit, *v.*	तुखाना *tukháná.*	थूकना.
Spittle, *n.*	उच्चूल *uchchúl.*	थूक.
Split, *v. i.*	पैयाना *páiyáná.*	चिर जाना.
— *v. t.*	पैहताना *páihatáná.*	चीरना.
Spoon, *n.*	सुकुर *sukur.*	डवर, दखी.
Spread, *v.*	तार्सी सीश्राना *tàrsí síáná*, श्रोरसहताना *orsahtáná.*	बिछाना, फैलाना.
— out grain, *v.*	रीकाना *ríkáná.*	अनाज फैलाना.
Squirrel, *n.*	चिडराल *chiḍrál.*	गिलहरी.
Stand, *v.*	निताना *nitáná.*	खड़ा होना.
— (make to) *v.*	निलहताना *nilahtáná.*	खड़ा करना.
Star, *n.*	जुनियां *juniyáṇ*, सुकुम *sukum.*	तारे.
Steal, *v.*	कल्लीना *kalliná.*	चुराना.
Stem, *n.*	वुडूम *wuḍúm.*	डंठा, बोंट.
Stick, *n.*	वड़िया *waṛiyá.*	छड़ी.
— *v. i.*	जिर्कसाना *jirksáná*, पचिहताना *pachihtáná.*	फस जाना.
Stink, *v.*	दैंगाना *dáiṇgáná.*	दुर्गन्धी होना.
Stir, *v.*	दुर्साना *dursáná.*	सरकाना, मथना.
Stomach, *n.*	पीर *pír.*	पेट.
Stone, *n.*	टोंगी *ṭoṇgí.*	पत्थर.

English.	Gondi.	Hindi.
Stones for cooking with, *n.*	सदोली *sadolí.*	चूल्हा.
Stool, *n.*	कुत्तुल *kuttul.*	पीढ़ी, माची.
Stoop, *v.*	मुर्साना *mursáná.*	झुकना.
Storm, *n.*	धूका *dhúká,* झकर *jhakar.*	आन्धी.
Story, *n.*	वेसेड़ी *weseṛí.*	कहानी.
Straw, *n.*	पीड़ी *piṛí.*	पुआल, पैरा.
—— a, *n.*	कोला *kolá.*	पुआल का एक तिन्का.
Strife, *n.*	कैजा *káijá.*	लड़ाई.
Strike (a tent), *v.*	अरहताना *arahtáná.*	डेरा गिराना.
String, *n.*	नूल *núl.*	सूत.
Such, *pron., adj.*	ईताल *ítál.*	ऐसा.
Suck, *v.*	ऊतीना *útíná.*	चूसना.
Suddenly, *adv.*	बड़साने *baṛsáne.*	अचानक, एका एकी.
Suffer (only used with 'hunger and thirst'), *v.*	अस्साना *assáná.*	लगना (प्यास या भूख).
Sun, *n.*	सूरियाल *súriyál.*	सूरज.
Sunshine, *n.*	अद्दी *addí.*	धूप.
Surely, *adv.*	मुकुर *mukur.*	निहसंदेह.
Swallow, *v.*	रोपाना *ropáná.*	निगलना.
Sweep, *v.*	सैयाना *sáiyáná.*	झाड़ना.
Sweet-smelling, *adj.*	माहकार *máhkár.*	सुगन्ध.
Swell, *v.*	तोईयाना *toiyáná.*	फूल जाना.

English.	Gondi.	Hindi.
Tail, *n.*	तोकार *tokár.*	पूंछ.
Take, *v.*	येताना *yetáná.*	लेना.
—— away, *v.*	वोईना *woíná.*	ले जाना.
—— out, *v.*	तन्दाना *tandáná.*	निकालना.
Tall, *adj.*	ढोंगल *ḍhoṇgal.*	लम्बा, ऊंचा.
Tamarind tree (*Tamarindus Indica*), *n.*	सित्ता *sittá,* छित्ता *chhittá.*	इमली.
Tank, *n.*	बोड्डी *boḍḍí.*	तलाव, ताल.
Taste, *v.*	वण्डीना *waṇḍíná.*	चीखना.
Teach, *v.*	करहताना *karahtáná,* केंचहताना *keṇchahtáná.*	सिखाना, सुनाना.
Teak tree (*Tectona grandis*), *n*	टेका *ṭeká.*	सागून.
Tear (rent), *n.*	काड़ेहक *káṛehak.*	चिर.
Tear, *v.*	सर्रहताना *sarrahtáná.*	चीरना, फाड़ना.
Teat, *n.*	अड़ील *aṛíl.*	थन.
Ten (number).	पद *pad.*	दस.
Tender, *adj.*	कनरो *kanaro.*	कोमल.
Tendu tree (*Diospyros Melanoxylon*) *n.*	तुमरी *tumarí.*	अबनूस.
That, *pron.*	अद *ad.*	वह (नपुनसक लिंग)
Thatch, *v.*	वेसाना *wesáná.*	छाना.

English.	Gondi.	Hindi.
Thatcher, *n.*	वेसे *wese.*	छानेवाला.
Thee, *pron.*	नीकुन *níkun.*	तुझको.
Their, *pron.*	ओर्कना *orkná.*	उनका.
Then, *adv.*	अस्के *aske.*	तब.
Thence.	हुन्दाल *hundál.*	वहां से.
There, *adv.*	अग्गा *aggá.*	वहां.
Therefore, *adv.*	इदेन लाने *iden láne.*	इस लिये.
They, *pron.*	ओर्क *ork.*	वे.
Thicket, *n.*	पतेरा *paterá.*	गझिन जंगल, या [बन.
Thief, *n.*	कल्ले *kalle,* कल्वाल *kalwál.*	चोर.
Thigh, *n.*	करकी *karkí.*	जांघ.
Thirst, *n.*	येत्क *yetk.*	प्यास.
——— *v.*	येत्क अस्साना *yetk* [*assáná.*	प्यासा होना.
This, *pron.*	एर *er,* इद *id.*	यह.
Thistle, *n.*	कटाइन *kaṭáin.*	भटकटैया.
Thither, *adv.*	हक्के *hakke.*	उधर.
Those, *pron.*	औ *ou.*	वे.
Thou, *pron.*	इम्मा *immá.*	तू.
Thread, *v.*	काचाना *kácháná.*	गूथना.
Three (number)	मूण्ड *múṇḍ.*	तीन.
Thresh, *v.*	विस्सीना *wissíná.*	गाहना.
Threshing-floor [*n.*	कड़ा *kaṛá.*	खलिहान.
Throat, *n.*	वरेर *warer,* घुटकी [*ghuṭkí.*	गला.
Tile (broken), *n.*	पिड़क *piṛak,* पिन्का [*pinká.*	टूटा हुआ खपड़ा.
Tilli-grain (milt) [*n.*	नूंग *núṇg.*	तिल्ली.

English.	Gondi.	Hindi.
Tired (to be), *v.*	दोरीना *doríná.*	थक जाना.
Tire another (to)	दोरसहताना *dorsah-*	थकाना.
To-day, *n.* [*v.*	नेर *ner.* [*táná.*	आज.
Token, *n.*	ठोंका *ṭhoṇká.*	सैन, चिन्ह.
Tongue, *n.*	वन्जेर *wanjer.*	जीभ.
Tooth, *n.*	पल *pal.*	दांत.
Torch, *n.*	सूर *súr.*	डामर.
Touch, *v. t.*	इट्टाना *iṭṭáná.*	छूना.
Tread, *v. t.*	जारीना *járíná.*	रौंदना.
Tree, *n.*	मरा *mará.*	पेड़.
Tremble, *v.*	कसंगीना *kasaṇgíná,* कसंगिताना *kasaṇgitáná.*	कांपना, थरथराना.
Tribe, *n.*	पारी *párí.*	गोत्र.
Trouble, *v.*	विट्टे कीआना *wiṭṭe*	दुख देना.
Trough, *n.* [*n.*	डोंगा *ḍoṇgá.* [*kíáná.*	डोंगा, डोंगी. [नल.
Tube in oil-press	पिटला *piṭlá.*	तेल निचोड़ने का
Turmeric, *n.*	कमका *kamká.*	हलदी.
Turn, *v. i.*	वलीताना *walítáná.*	घूमना.
—— *v. t.*	तिरहताना *tirahtáná*	घुमाना.
—— back, *v. t.*	मल्लहताना *mallahtá-*	लौटाना.
Twin, *n.*	येमाल *yemál.* [*ná.*	यमक, यमल.
Two, *num.*	रण्ड *raṇḍ.*	दो.
Umbrella (of leaves), *n.*	कालो *kálo.*	पत्तों का छाता.

English.	Gondi.	Hindi.
Umbrella (ordinary, *n.*)	छानी *chhání.*	छाता.
Upon, *prep.*	परों *parroṇ.*	पर.
Urine, *n.*	नर्कुल *narkul.*	मूत, मूत्र.
Us, *pron.*	माकुन *mákun.*	हमको.
Vegetable, *n.*	कुसरी *kusrí.*	तरकारी, साग.
— (cooked), *n.*	चकना *chakná.*	पकी हुई तरकारी.
Vein, *n.*	चीरा *chírá.*	नाड़ी.
Verandah, *n.*	परछी *parchhí.*	परछी.
Vetch, *n.*	पुरपुल *purpul.*	उर्द.
Village, *n.*	नार *nár.*	गांव.
Virago, *n.*	डोंड़हरे *ḍonṛhare.*	लड़ाकी.
Voice, *n.*	लेंग *leṇg.*	शब्द.
Waist, *n.* [*n.*	नन्नी *nanní.*	कमर.
— cloth (men's)	गांडाल *gánḍál.*	धोती.
— —(women's)	आचुल *áchul.*	साड़ी.
Wait, *v.* [*n.*	पोसाना *posáná.*	ठहरना.
Walk, *v.*	ताकाना *tákáná.*	चलना.
— (cause to), *v.*	ताकसहताना *táksah-táná.* [*kíáná.*	चलाना.
— (slowly), *v.*	गोस्ली कीआना *goslí*	धीरे चलना.
Wander, *v.*	तिड़िताना *tiṛitáná.*	घूमना.
Warm, *adj.* [*v.*	कास्ताल *kástál.*	गरम.
——— (oneself),	आराना *áráná.*	तापना.

English.	Gondi.	Hindi.
Wash, *v.*	नुर्राना *nurráná*, नुर्सी येना *nursí yená.* [tatáná.	धोना.
— (clothes), *v.*	सुकसी तताना *suksí*	कपड़े धोके लेआना.
Watch, *v. t.*	केपाना *kepáná.*	रखाना.
Water, *n.*	येर *yer.*	पानी.
Wax (of ear), *n.*	कोरंगेड *koraṇgeḍ.*	कान का खूंट.
Way, *n.*	सरी *sarí.*	राह, मार्ग.
We, *pron.*	मम्माट *mammáṭ*, मम्माड़ *mammáṛ.*	हम.
Weak, *adj.* [*v.*	सीरतोर *sírtor.*	दुर्बल.
Weave together	किच्चाना *kichcháná.*	गूथके बनाना.
Web, *n.*	कुस्सो *kusso.*	जाला.
Wedding, *n.*	मड़मीं *maṛmíṇ.*	बिवाह.
Weep, *v.*	अड़ाना *aṛáná.*	रोना.
Weevil, *n.* [*adj.*	नूसी *núsí.*	घुन.
Well (of health),	नहना *nahaná.*	अच्छी तरह से, अच्छा
Wet, *adj.*	पाहनाल *páhnál.*	गीला.
— (to be), *v.*	नांदाना *náṇḍáná.*	भीगना.
What? *pron.*	बाल *bál.*	क्या.
When, *adv.*	अस्के *aske.*	जब.
When? *adv.*	बस्के *baske.*	कब.
Whence? *adv.*	बग्गाहड़ा *baggáhaṛá*, बग्गाटाल *baggá-*	कहां से.
Where? *adv.*	बग्गा *baggá.* [*ṭál.*	कहां.
Wherever, *adv.*	बगने *bagane.*	जहां कहीं.

English.	Gondi.	Hindi.
Whiskers, *n.*	कट्टे *kaṭṭe.*	गाल मोंछा.
Whistle, *n.*	सीसरी *sísarí.*	सीती.
White, *adj.*	पण्ड़री *paṇṛarí,* उजरो *ujaro.*	उजला.
Whitewash, *n.*	चुई *chuí.*	चूना.
Whither? *adv.*	बेक *bek,* बिक्के *bikke.*	किधर.
Who? *pron.*	बोर *bor.*	कौन.
Whom? *pron.*	बोन *bon.*	किसको.
Why? *adv.*	बारी *bárí.*	क्यों.
Wife, *n.*	माइजू *máijú.*	पतनी.
—'s brother, [*n.*	सेरेन्दू *serrandú.*	साला.
Wild, *adj.*	खेड़ा *kheṛá.*	बनैला, जंगली.
Wind, *n.*	वरी *warí.*	हवा.
Winnow, *v.*	तुरेहताना *turehtáná.*	उसाना.
Wine, *n.*	दारंगा *dáraṇgá,* कल *kal.*	मदिरा.
Wipe, *v.*	उस्माना *usmáná.*	पोंछना.
Wish, *v.*	पड़कीना *paṛkíná.*	चाहना.
Within, *prep.*	रोपा *ropá.*	भीतर.
Wolf, *n.*	बोधाल *bodhál.*	भेड़िया, हुंड़ार.
Woman, *n.*	आर *ár.*	स्त्री.
— who forces a man to take her to wife.	सैवारी *sáiwárí.*	जो पुरुष के घर में व्याह करने को घुस जाती है.
—'s female friend.	सांगो *sáṇgo.*	सखी.

English.	Gondi.	Hindi.
Wood, *n.*	कटिया *kaṭiyá.*	लकड़ी.
World(upper), *n*	जामू दीप *jámú díp.*	परलोक.
—— (this), *n.*	सिंगार दीप *siṇgár díp.*	इसलोक.
—— (lower), *n.*	अलोप दीप *alop díp.*	पाताल.
Worm, *n.*	पुड़ी *puṛí.*	कीड़ा.
Worship (in, to bury eggs)	डाबुर जीसहताना *ḍábur jísahtáná.*	पूजा में अंडों को गाड़ देना.
Wound, *n.*	करम *karam.*	घांव.
Wrist, *n.*	मुरुआ *muruá.*	कलाई, गट्टा.
Yawn, *n.*	वही *wahí.*	जमहाई.
Years, *n.*	वरसां *warsáṇ.*	वरसां.
Year (this), *n.*	येंड़ *yeṇṛ.*	आसों.
—— (last), *n.*	नीरे *níre.*	उस बरस.
Yes, *adv.*	इंगे *iṇge.*	हां.
Yesterday, *n.*	निन्ने *ninne.*	कल.
You, *pron.*	इम्माट *immáṭ*, इम्माड़ *immáṛ.*	तुम.
Young (of animals), *n.*	चीवाल *chíwál.*	बच्चा.
—— (man), *n.*	रप्पोड़ *rappoṛ.*	जवान.
Your, *pron.*	मीवोर *míwor*, मीवा *míwá.*	तुम्हारा, तुम्हारी.

EXAMPLES OF SHORT GONDI SENTENCES.

बोर बारी किलीतातोर *bor bárí kilítátor.* Who is calling out? and why?

बारां इम्मा इदेन वहता पोरीतोनी *báráṇ immá iden wahtá porítoní.* Are you able to explain this?

नाकुन कूर कूसनाके इग्गाहड़ा हन्दाले आयाल *nákun kúr kúsnáke iggáhaṛá handále áyál.* I must start from here at cock-crow.

केंछी इर्राड़ *keṇchhí irráṛ.* Listen attentively.

नर्का कुड़ो ते पुलियाल बाहुन किलीन्द इम्माड़ केंजतीड़ धों हिल्ले *narká kuṛo te puliyál báhun kilínd ímmáṛ keṇj-tíṛ dhoṇ hille.* How the tiger was calling out at night in the hill! did you hear or not?

कोपा ना नेदे वल्ले वियार पिरता ओर अहताले वोसहतानुर *kopá ná nede walle wiyár pirtá or ahtále wo-sahtánur.* In Kopá's field much rubbish has sprung up, he is going to take men to root it up.

फागू इसारी रोते हिल्लेन्दुर ओर ओन मिरहकसोरे हत्तुर *Phágú isárí rote hillendur or on mirahksore hattur.* Phagu is not now in the house, he has gone to look for him.

पोइना इग्गा सैवारी नेंगता अनि तिन्नाके कमका दोस्ता *poiná iggá sáiwárí neṇgtá ani tinnáke kamká dostá.* A would-be wife has made her way into the head-man's house, and after eating has thrown turmeric on him.

पेड़गाल करसनाके अरसी हत्तुर *peṛgál karasnáke arsí hattur.* The boy playing has fallen down.

नीकुन तव्वीता धों हिल्ले *níkun tawwítá dhoṇ hille.* Can you see or not?

चरू ते येर तोरसेना *charú te yer torsená.* Pour (me) out water from the brass vessel.

धनिया तुन नुरसी नच्छुम *dhaniyá tun nursí nachchhum.* Clean out the plate.

नन्ना वेसीले जारी कुइयाका *nanná wesíle járí kuiyáká.* I will cut grass for thatching.

विच्छोके हन किलीसी तरा *wichchhoke han kilísí tará.* Run and call him here.

नवरियाल डाबुर जीसहताले वासी मत्तोर *Nawariyál ḍábur jísahtále wásí mattor.* Nawariyál had come to bury eggs (in poojah).

ओना येटी नत्तता *oná yeṭí natt'tá.* His goat has borne a young one.

निच्छी मन सांगो नन्ना सोई येत्कुन वायितोना, निलतोना *nichchhí man sáṇgo nanná soí yetkun wayitoná, niltoná.* Wait a moment, friend, I too am coming to fill water. (*Answer*) I am waiting.

सरापी येच्छीकुन रच्चा ऊसुम *sarápí yechchhíkun rachchá úsum.* Bring cow-dung and plaster the court-yard.

सवोटे छूछू नेंगता तान टंड़सुम *sawoṭe chhúchhú neṇgtá tán ṭaṇṛsum.* A musk-rat has got among the salt, take it out.

नावा वानाके इम्मा पोसा *náwá wánáke immá posá.* Wait till I come.

सरपूह्क करीले हन्जी मत्तोरम *sarpúhk karíle hanjí mattoram.* We had gone to put on our shoes.

सरदे हन्नाके ओर मुलोल छौवा पन्तुर *sarde hannáke or mulol chhouwá pantur.* Going along the road he found a young hare.

टाली पाल ऊहतानुर *ṭálí pál úhtánur.* He will give (you) to drink cow's milk.

जावा वैसीत उन्नेंकं वायोरे *jáwá wáisít unneṇk wáyore.* The *penjh* is cooked, (but) those to drink it have not come.

नावा ननतुन बाल आता *náwá nantun bál átá.* What has happened to my loins?

ओर कत्तुर नन्ना कोठी ओहची कहची सीतान बाहे आयी नन्ना पुन्नोन *or kattur nanná koṭhí ohchí kahchí sítán báhe áyí nanná punnon.* He said, I have burst the granaries and measured (the grain); whatever be wrong, I know nothing of it.

पिटला ते नूंगनी टंड़तुर *piṭlá te núṇgní ṭaṇṛtur.* He has taken the tilli-oil from the oil-stick.

अग्गाहड़ा तल्हकदान बाल किएना *aggáhaṛá talhk'dán bál kiená.* I asked for it from there, what else could I do.

पोइना इग्गा कोष्टार वातां *poiná iggá koshtár wátáṇ.* Hindu women have come to the head-man's house.

कोइताह्क कल उन्जीकुन येंदानूं *koitáhk kal unjíkun yeṇdánúṇ.* Gond women drinking wine will dance.

नीवा इद परोल बोर वीसतुर *níwá id parol bor wístur.* Who gave you this name?

कलवाल नारी कलसी वोतुर *kalwál nárí kalsí wotur.* A thief yesterday, stealing, carried (it) off.

पद्दी यटींना रोपा मेहताता *paddí yeṭíṇná ropá mehtútá.* A pig is feeding among the goats.

कोपाल भांड़ी उघे कालतोर *kopál bháṇṛí ughe káltor.* The herdsman is collecting his dues.

नाल्क धियां आतुं ओन अर्की बैता *nálk dhiyáṇ átuṇ on arkí báitá.* He has had fever for four days.

ओना कन तेदतुं *oná kan tedtúṇ.* His eyes are inflamed.

इम्मा करूं मिन्नी सायिमा *immá karrú minne sáyimá.* Do not die of hunger.

ओन येत्क अस्ता *on yetk astá.* He is thirsty.

नावा पिर नोयुन्द *náwá pir noyund.* My stomach was aching.

ओर विच्छोरे बयाल ते मीड़ सीतुर *or wichchhore bayál te míṛ sítur.* Running he fell down in the hemp.

अरमी दामनी तुन उरेंहचीकुनं डैसाल *armí dámní tun urrahchíkun ḍáisál.* The buffalo breaking its rope will run away.

पाल पीरा कासहची इर्रा *pál pírá kásahchí irrá.* Milk the cow, and warm and put away the milk.

नन्ना मीकुन वहतातोना इस्सुर ईताल बप्पोरे केमाड़ *nanná míkun wahtátoná issur ítál bappore kemáṛ.* I am explaining (it) to you, so never do so again.

इद आयि पोरीताता पे अद हिल्ले आयि परो *id áyi porítátá pe ad hille áyi paro.* This is possible, but that is not possible.

नाटे मन्मा *náṭe manmá.* Don't remain in the villages.

इम्मा बोनी आन्दी *immá boní ándí.* Who are you? *or*, Where are you from?

बग्गाटोर कोसुर मी नाटे वान्दुर *baggáṭor kosur mí náṭe wándur.* From what place were the Hindus who came into your village.

पिर्र अराता *pirr arátá.* Rain falls.

गाज मिरसीलता *gáj mirsíltá.* Lightning is flashing.

माव्क नांदीतां *máwk náṇḍítáṇ.* The deer are getting wet.

बोर वहेर *bor waher.* Who could tell.

पिंडी नोरा *piṇḍí norá.* Grind the wheat.

सारी सुर्रा *sárí surrá.* Bake the bread.

वलीना वलीनाके नन्ना दोरसी हत्तान *walíná walínáke nanná dorsí hattán.* Going about hither and thither, I got tired.

दिकड़ी तारा *dikaṛí tárá.* Spread the clothes.

ओर बस्के आतुर *or baske átur.* When was he born?

अद अवेटे हिल्ले पोद्दो *ad aweṭe hille poddo.* There was no room for it in that.

ओरून पाटा वारीले बोर करहतुर *orún páṭá wáríle bor karrahtur.* Who taught them to sing songs?

बाहे आयेर नन्ना हनेना *báhe áyer nanná hanená.* I go whatever happens.

नीकुन बाल आता अद कियातोनी इद हिल्ले केवी *níkun bál átá ad kiyátoní id hille kewí.* What has come to you! you do that and don't do this.

ओना लेंग इग्गाहड़ा केंच्छी अरीता *oná leṇg iggáhará kenchchhí arrátá.* His voice makes itself heard from here.

नन्ना वोसी अवहन्दान *nanná wosí awahandán.* I took (it) away and conveyed (it) there.

वल्ले नर्का आसीत *walle narká ásít.* Many nights have passed.

इंगा कूरकी वायिताता *iṇgá kúrkí wáyitátá.* Now sleep is coming (over him).

हन्ते सुन्जा *hante sunjá.* Go and sleep.

अद्देनोर मोइदो तान पोहची सीतुर *addenor moido tán pohchí sítur.* Her husband has deserted her.

कोरियार मियार रन्डे कीन्दूं *koriyár miyár ranḍe kíndúṇ.* The daughter-in-law and daughter both did (it).

कुर कूसीता *kur kúsítá.* The cock crows.

नै मुहचीता *nái muhchítá.* The dog barks.

मल येदींता *mal yediṇtá.* The peacock dances.

गाटो अट्टीता *gáṭo aṭṭitá.* She cooks the rice.

येर निहताता *yer nihtátá.* She draws water.

दिकड़ी सराता *dikṛí sarrátá.* The cloth is rending.

सूर बोत्तीता *súr bottitá.* The torch is burning.

पीनी अस्सीता *píní assítá.* It is cold.

अद्दी तराता *addí tarrátá.* It is hot.

मम्माट आरतम *mammáṭ ártam.* We have warmed ourselves.

इम्माड़ आरन्दीड़ *immáṛ árandíṛ.* You were warming yourselves.

सेनाल लकन्दा वातुर दोरतुर आतेके इंगा ओर रोमीतोर *senál lakandá wátur dortur áteke iṇgá or romítor.* The old man came from far, he is wearied with coming, now he is resting.

ओर तनवा येटीन ममदुर साधु तेन रण्ड रूपयान्क येतुर *or tanwá yeṭín mamdur sádhu ten raṇạ rupayánk yetur.* He was selling his goat, the devotee got it for two rupees.

नन्ना कुड़ो ते कटियां नर्कीले दाका अनि पाउर आकी ततका *nanná kuṛo te kaṭiyáṇ narkíle dáká ani páur ákí tatká.* I am going to the hill to cut wood and to bring mahulain leaves.

नीवा कुर्क मेस्क दोस्ता मूण्ड मेस नाकुन सीसहचुम *níwá kurk mesk dostá múṇḍ mes nákun sísahchum.* Your fowl has laid eggs, give me three eggs.

कुरवी पोंगीता *kurwí poṇgítá.* The pitcher leaks.

नावा कोरका वराता *náwá korká warátá.* My cattle-shed leaks.

बोनई किलीसी तरा वेसी सानुर *bonaí kilísí tará wesí sánur.* Fetch someone to thatch it.

ओर जारी लक्कीले हन्जी मत्तोर *or járí lakkíle hanjí mattor.* He was going to count grass (bundles).

नन्ना केपीले हन्दातोना *nanná kepíle handátoná.* I am going to watch (my field).

जावा उन्डाले डोप्पा अनि गाटो तिन्दाले कूनी किचाड़ *jáwá unḍále ḍoppá ani gáṭo tindále kúní kichcháṛ.* Make a small plate of leaves for drinking *penjh* and a large one for eating rice.

नेदे वीतीले पुरपुल कहची वोयाकी *nede witíle purpul kahchí woyákí.* Measure out *urda* and take it for sowing in the field.

हूड़सोके मन *húṛsoke man.* Keep on the look-out.

मीन्क बैयाले ओर कट्टा दोहन्दुर पे दोहनाके ओरसीत *mínk báiyále or kaṭṭá dohandur pe dohanáke orsít.* He was fastening together a frame-work for catching fish, but in doing it it broke.

तला तर्गता रैगत हिल्ले *talá targtá ráigt hille.* My head pains me, it does not get better.

हिल्ले नहनई अर्की बैयुन *hille nahanaí arkí báiyun.* I am not well, I had fever.

नेर नारी पिर्र जिआर *ner nárí pirr jiár.* To-day or to-morrow rain will fall.

Printed by Gilbert & Rivington (Lim.), Clerkenwell Road, London.

Published by

Facsimile Publisher
Ashok Vihar, Delhi-110052 (India)
Website: www.facsimilepublishers.com

Distributed by

Gyan Books Pvt. Ltd.
5, Ansari Road, Daryaganj, New Delhi-110002 (India)
E-mail: books@gyanbooks.com, Website: www.gyanbooks.com

9 789333 383745